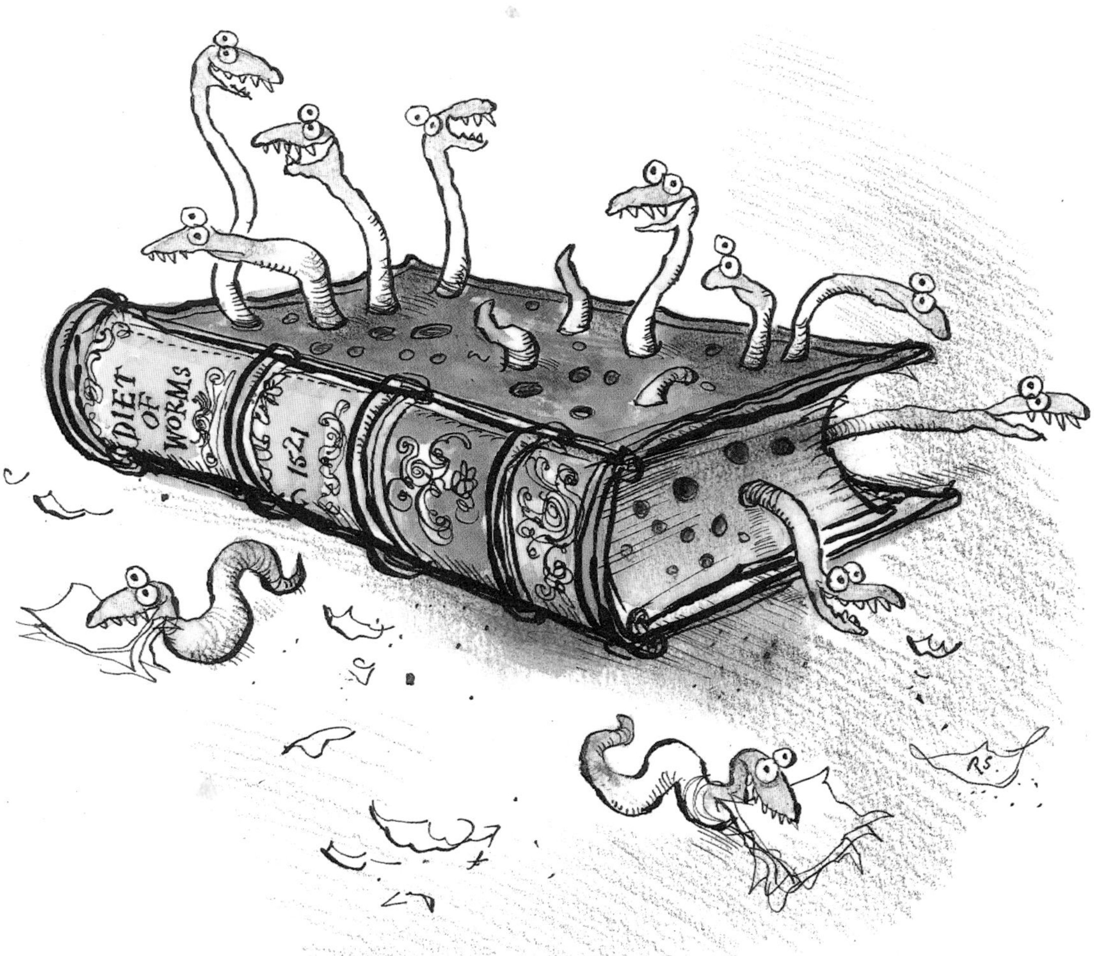
DIET OF WORMS
1521
RS.

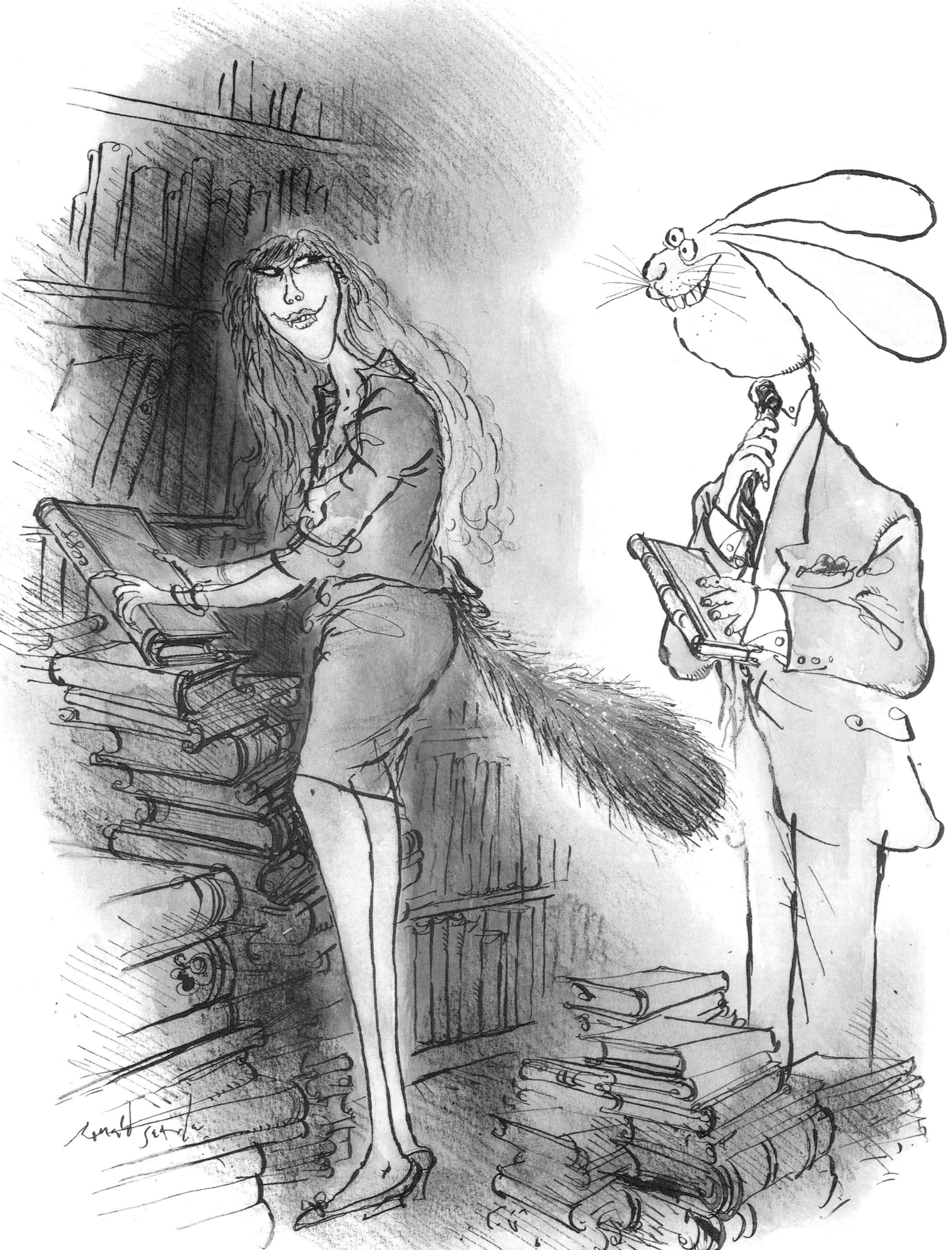

Slightly Foxed
–but still desirable

RONALD SEARLE'S

wicked world
of Book Collecting

SOUVENIR PRESS

First published 1989 by Souvenir Press Ltd,
43 Great Russell Street, London WC1B 3PA
and simultaneously in Canada

ISBN 0 285 62945 X

Typeset, printed and bound in Great Britain by
BPCC Hazell Books Ltd
Member of BPCC Ltd
Aylesbury, Bucks, England

Ever since as a child I lurked, lingered and slobbered in anticipation over the sixpenny book boxes of the Cambridge booksellers, I have never ceased to rummage wherever more than two books are brought together. In the nineteen-thirties, when Heffers was still in Petty Cury and still had a soul, when old David's stall, farther along by Peas Hill, was still administered by smelly old Gustave, every Saturday morning would see me hard at it, breathlessly embarking on the last great treasure hunt available to man and boy with only limited means but with uncontrollable acquisitive literary ambitions. By the time I was fourteen, my three-shelf library was worth at least four pounds two and sixpence, *and* it boasted Nina Hamnett's *Laughing Torso*, with all plates present—especially the torso one . . .

As for catalogues: whenever I managed to beg, take, or even pinch one on my rounds, my weekend was made. I would spend it alone in my room, lost to the world over items of such unspeakable exoticism that if an armful of delights from the most perfumed local harem had been offered to this pimply teenager on a golden dish, they would barely have received a third glance. As it was, my trembling fingers could hardly turn the pink, green, or wicked looking yellow pages as, in an ecstasy of anticipation, I would stumble into the enticements of the 'Miscellaneous' section, or 'This month's remainders' in which, happily, I did not yet feature. Such was the heady expectation of thrills to come. But alas, on my pocket money, most of them were as far out of my reach as was Deanna Durbin, whose picture often kept me awake at night.

Thus the rot set in . . .

Ten thousand bookshops and twenty thousand catalogues later, I lick my wounds, while all around me almost half a kilometre of books now groan from lack of space.

Ordering from a bookseller's catalogue without speaking the specialist language is about as dangerous as trying to chat up the promised-in-marriage daughter of a Corsican tax inspector, and the retribution about as swift. But when cutting the string of a newly-arrived parcel of books, tearing off the superficial wrapping of cornflake boxes surrounding ancient copies of the *Observer* and reaching the inner sanctum that conceals the treasure, one knows just how Howard Carter felt when he was about to enter the tomb of Tutankhamun. Then, and only then, are the full subtleties of language revealed.

The bookseller's interpretation of 'slightly bubbled', 'trivial soiling', 'a little chafed', 'some trifling discoloration', or 'minor worming', for example, can range from delicate underestimation of the depth of a wormhole, to liability to a five-year sentence for criminal misrepresentation. In between we have poetic licence, cynical salesmanship and downright bloody banditry, as only members of a *confrérie* can exercise it. Happily, the bandits, however well-connected, are the minority in this wicked world of book collecting and, so long as one realises that trying to interpret the signs is about as exact a science as trying to read the future in tea leaves, one is as safe as one will ever be when straining to calculate how many words might have been eaten by those small wormholes in leaves 1^8, K^2 and X^3.

Meanwhile I say a pox on your 'slightly foxed as usual' and the rest of the jargon. But I must admit I still find you extremely desirable.

R.S.

A little dog-eared but otherwise acceptable

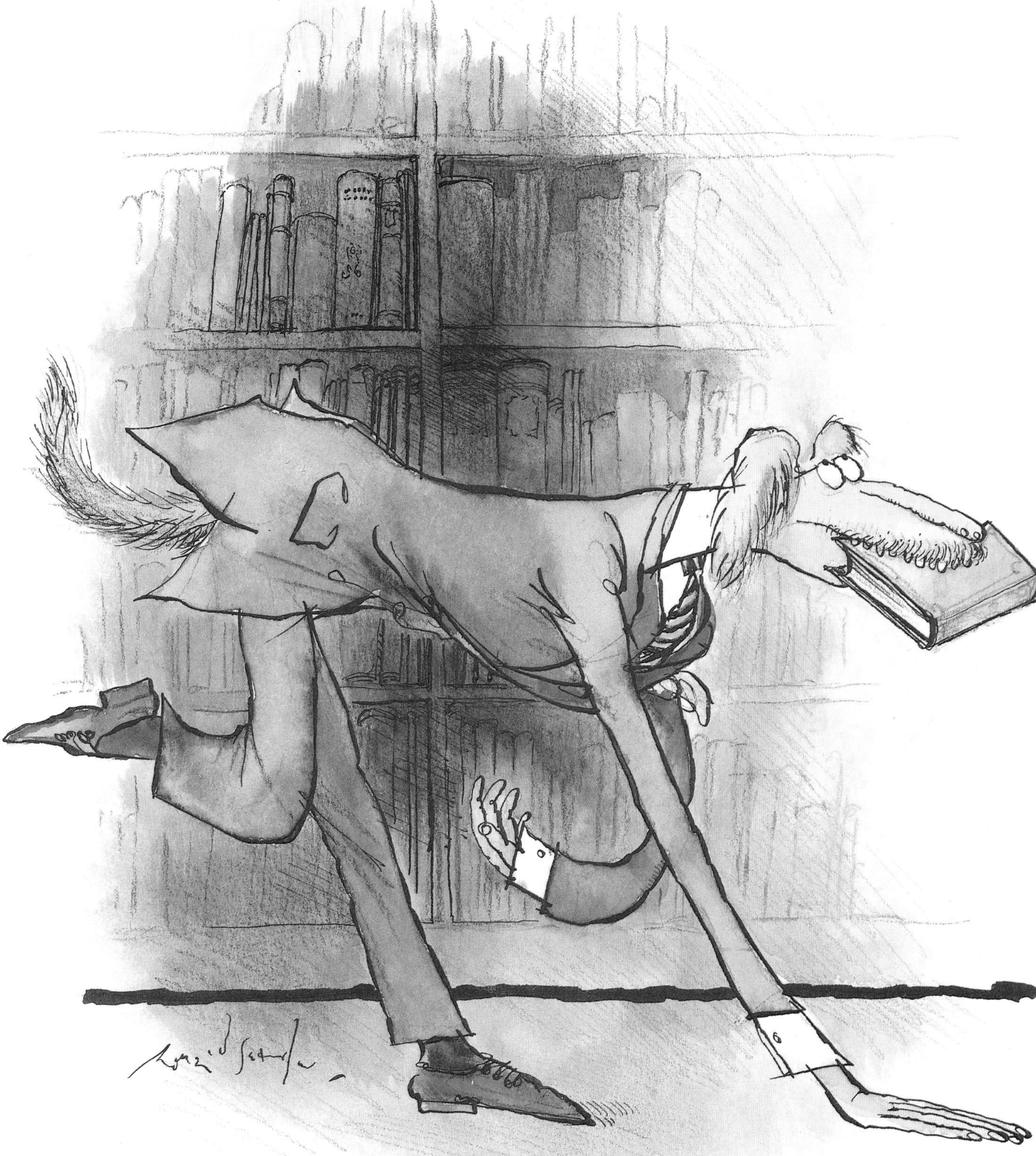

Extremities rubbed

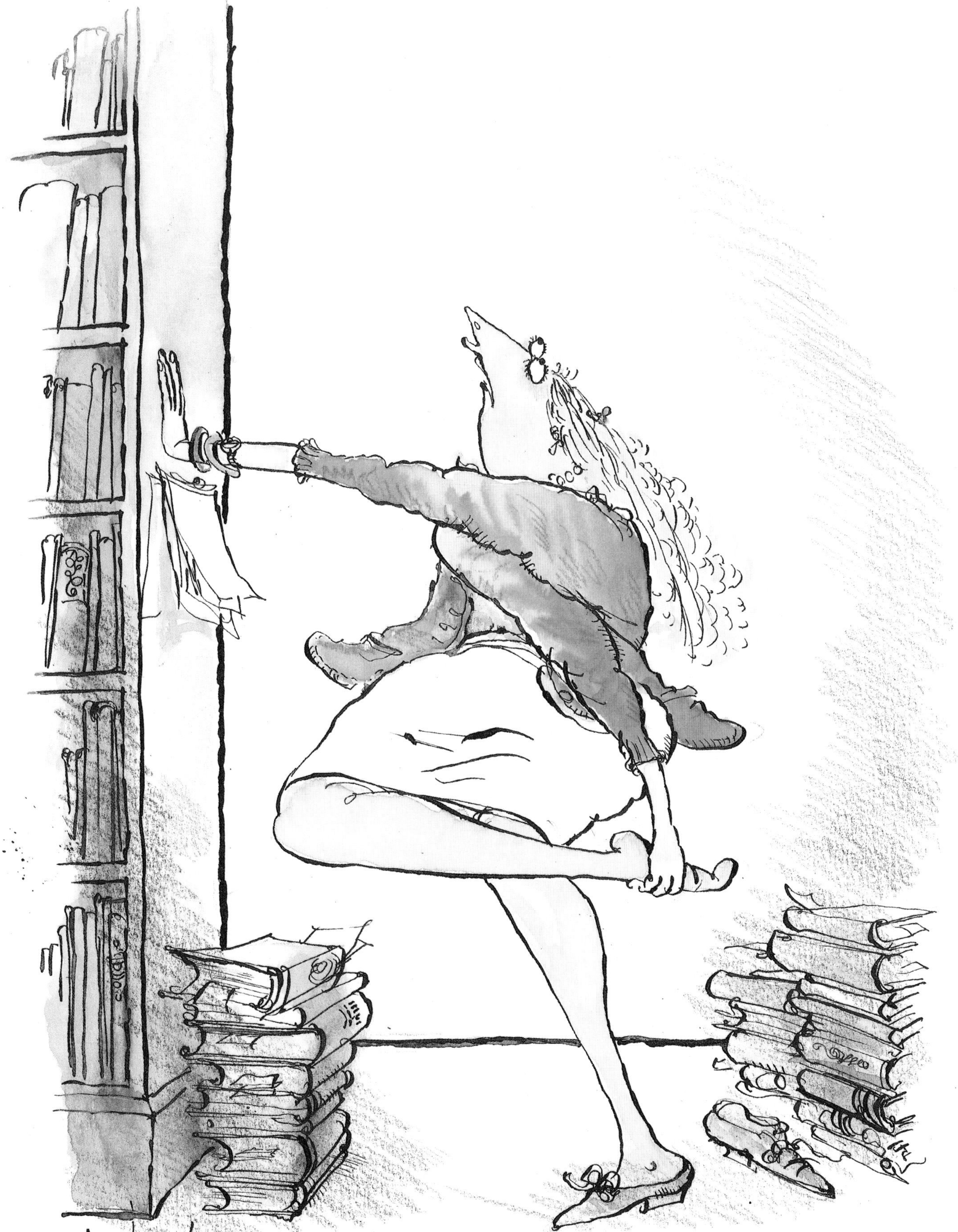

Old half roan

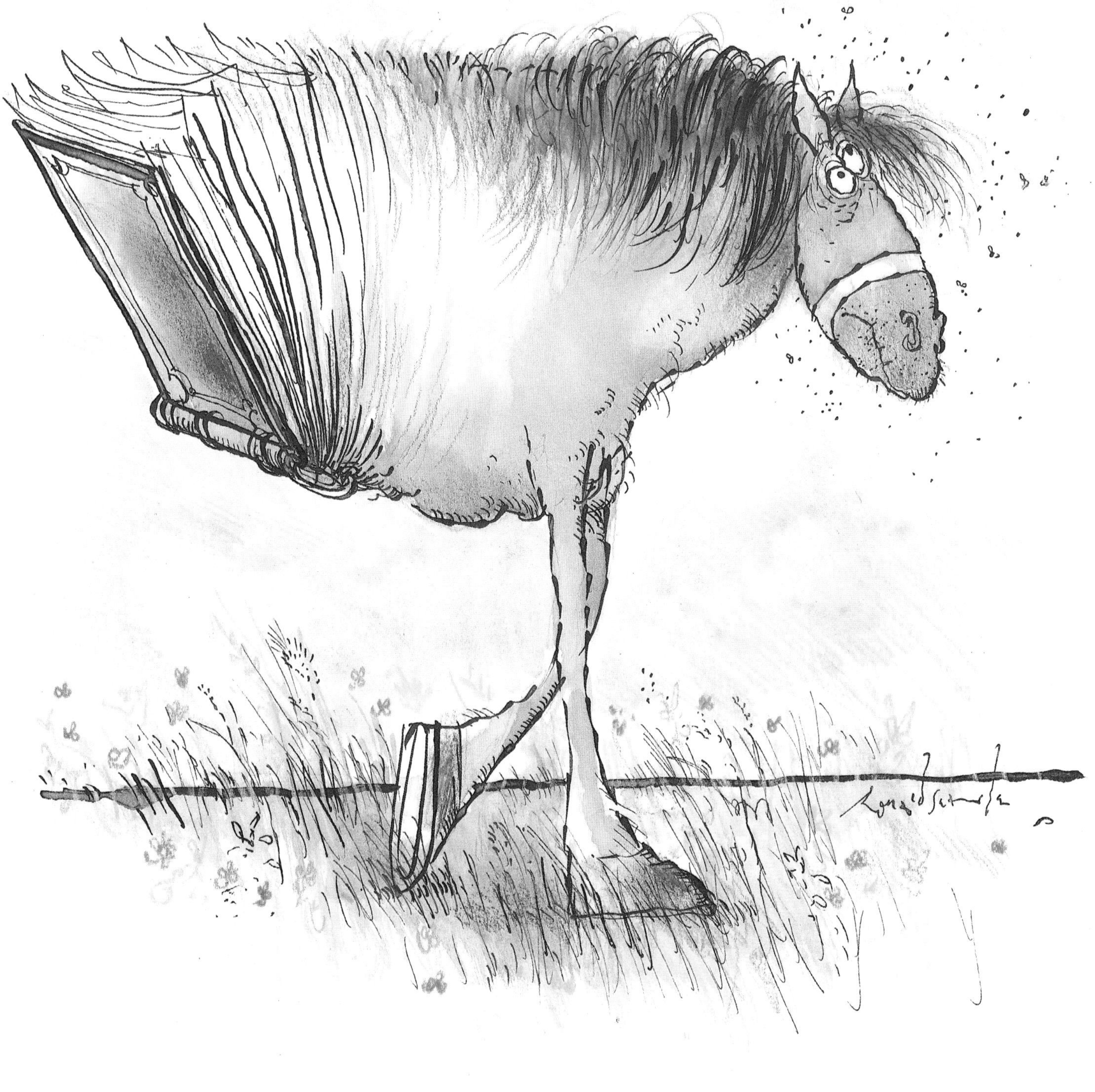

No copy in B.M.

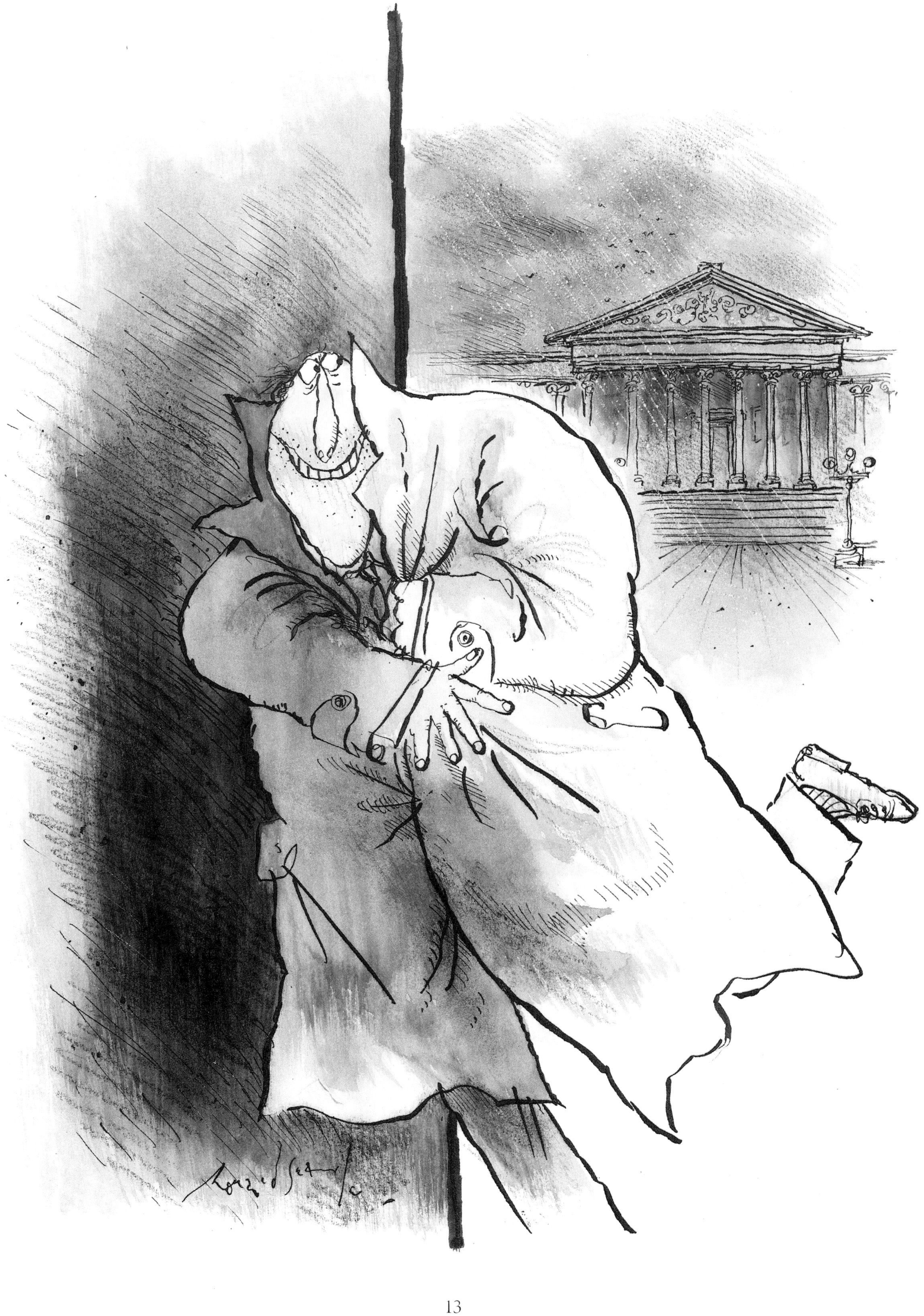

Evidence of some insect damage

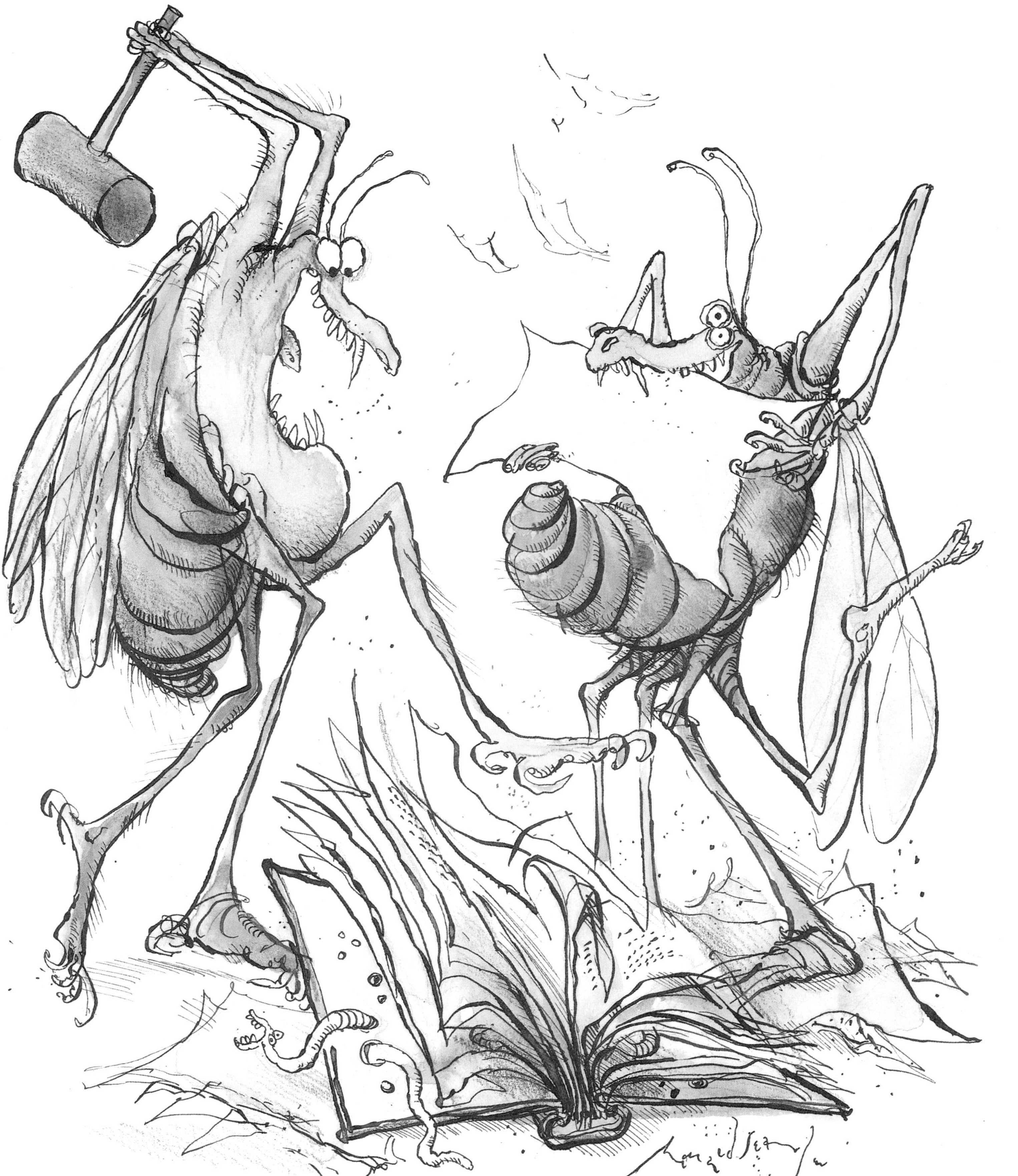

Worn and dusty

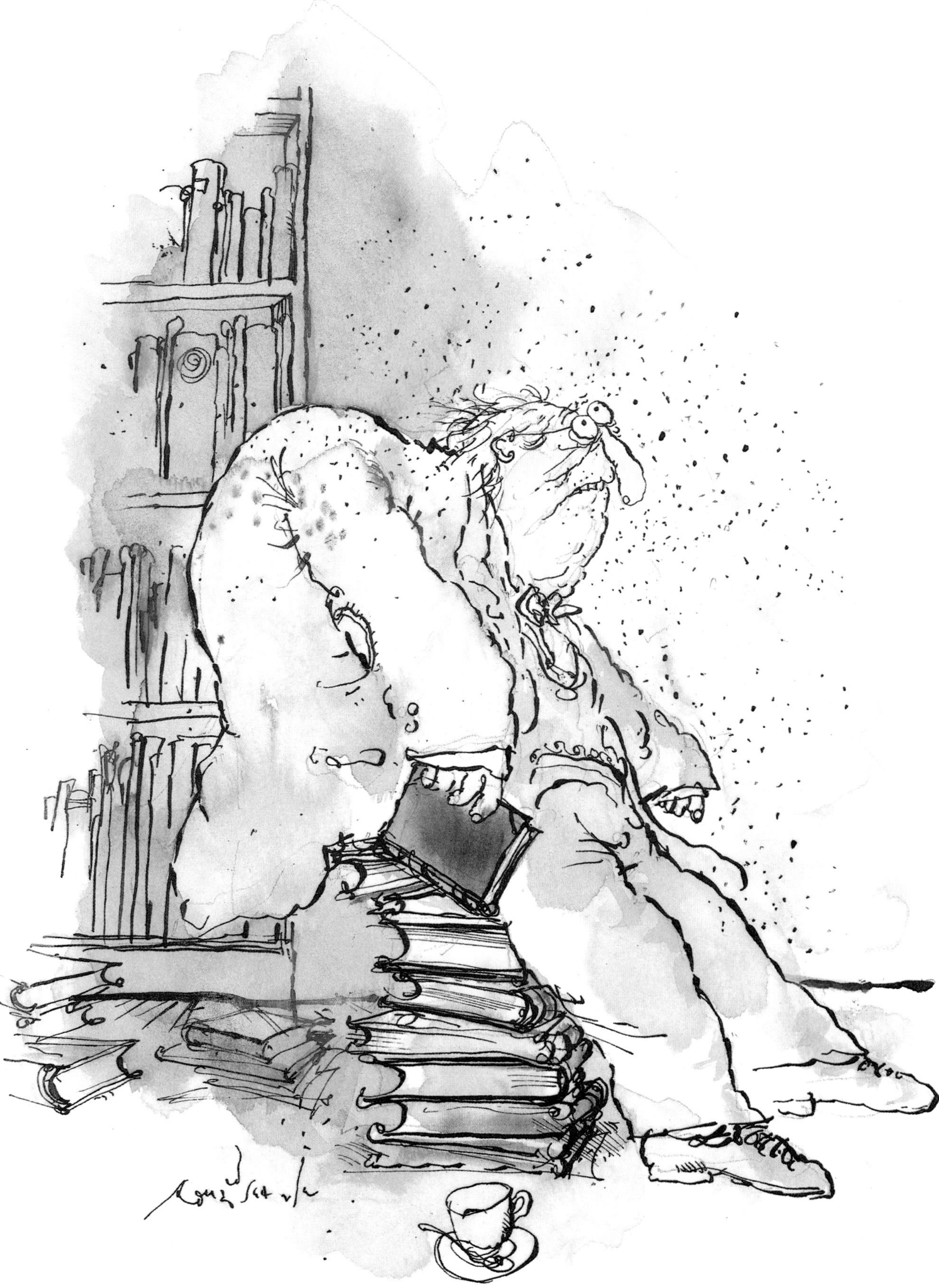

Frontispiece nicely mounted

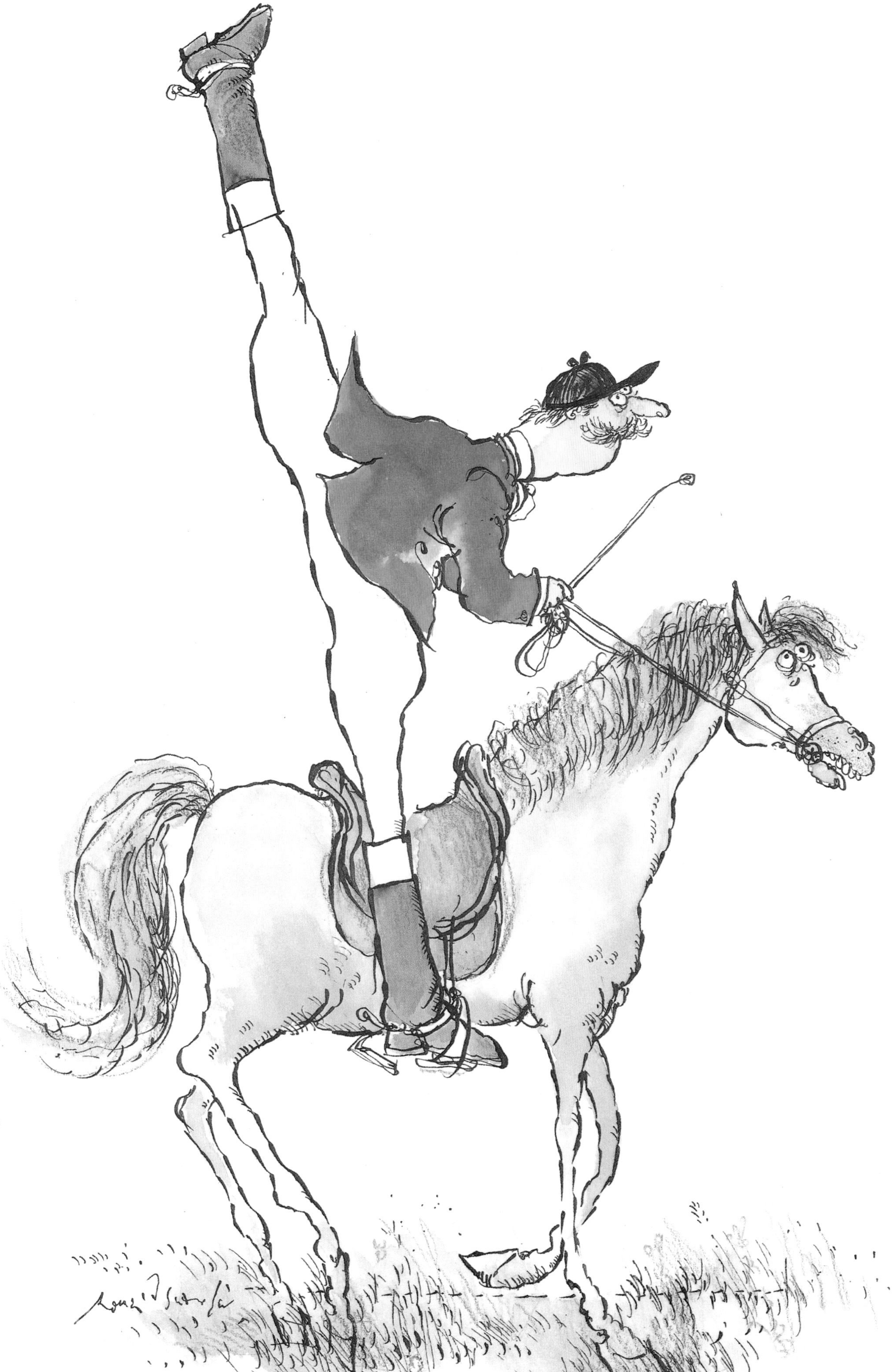

Very good in the original cloth

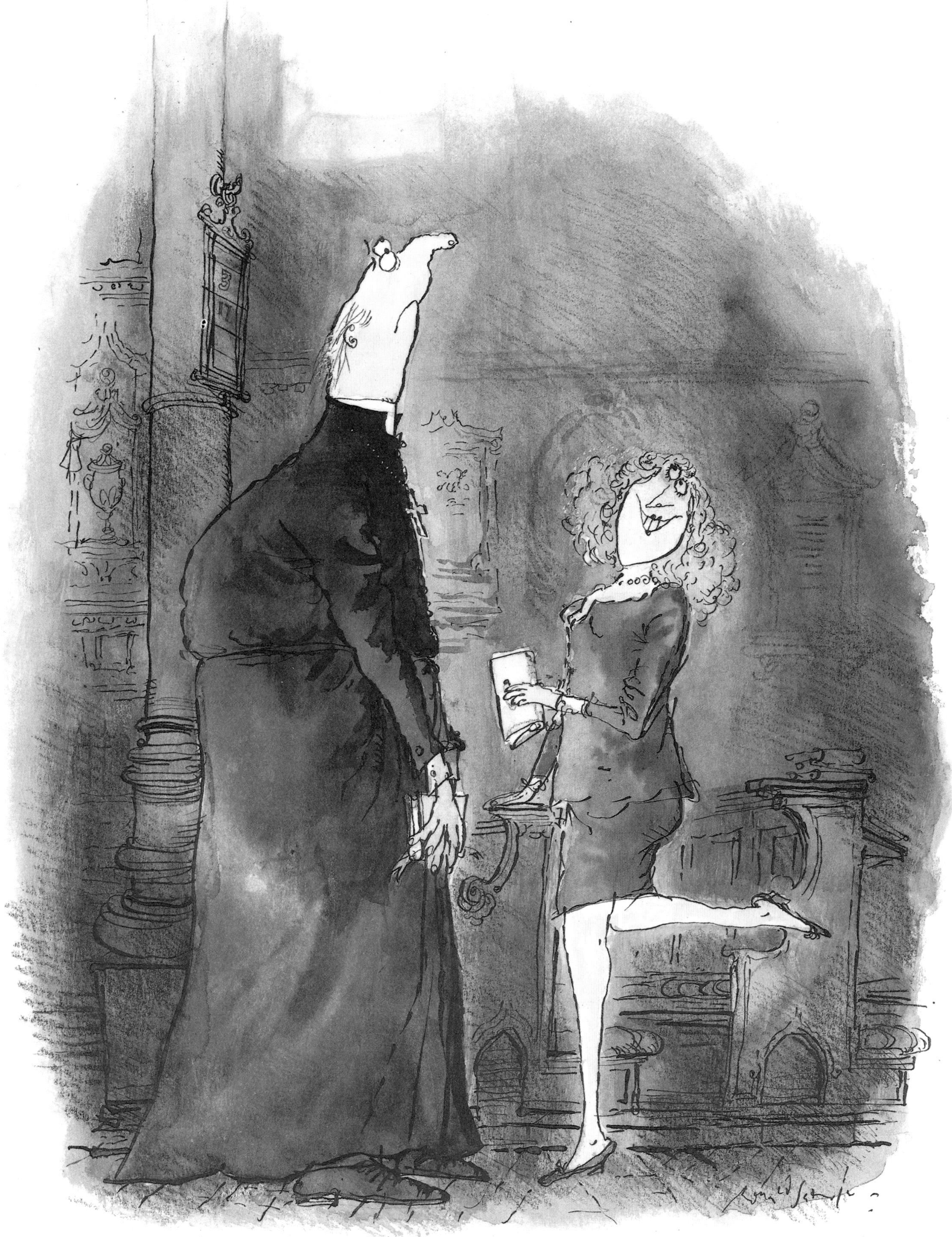

Contemporary sheep

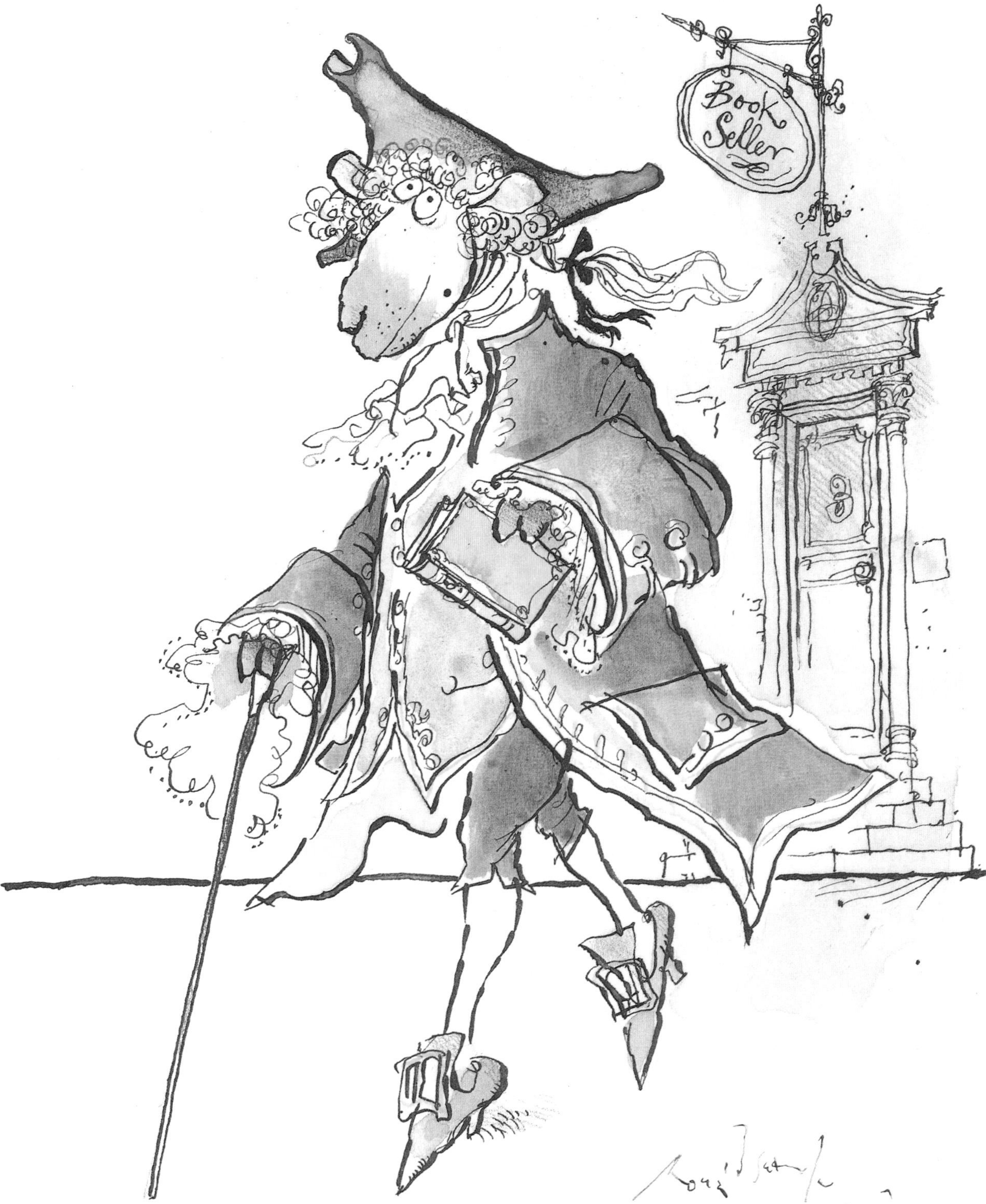
Book
Seller

Good working copy

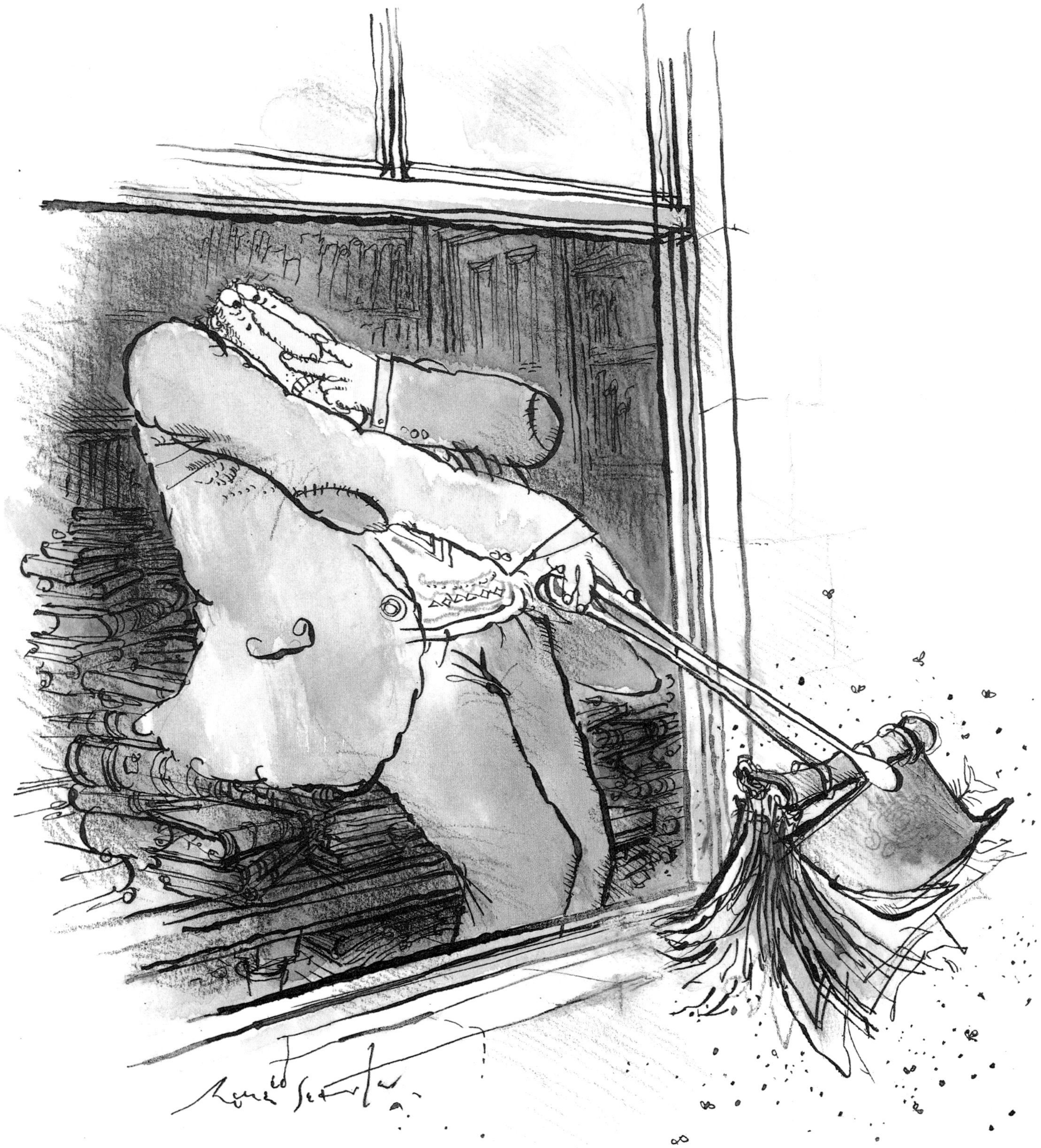

Half russia

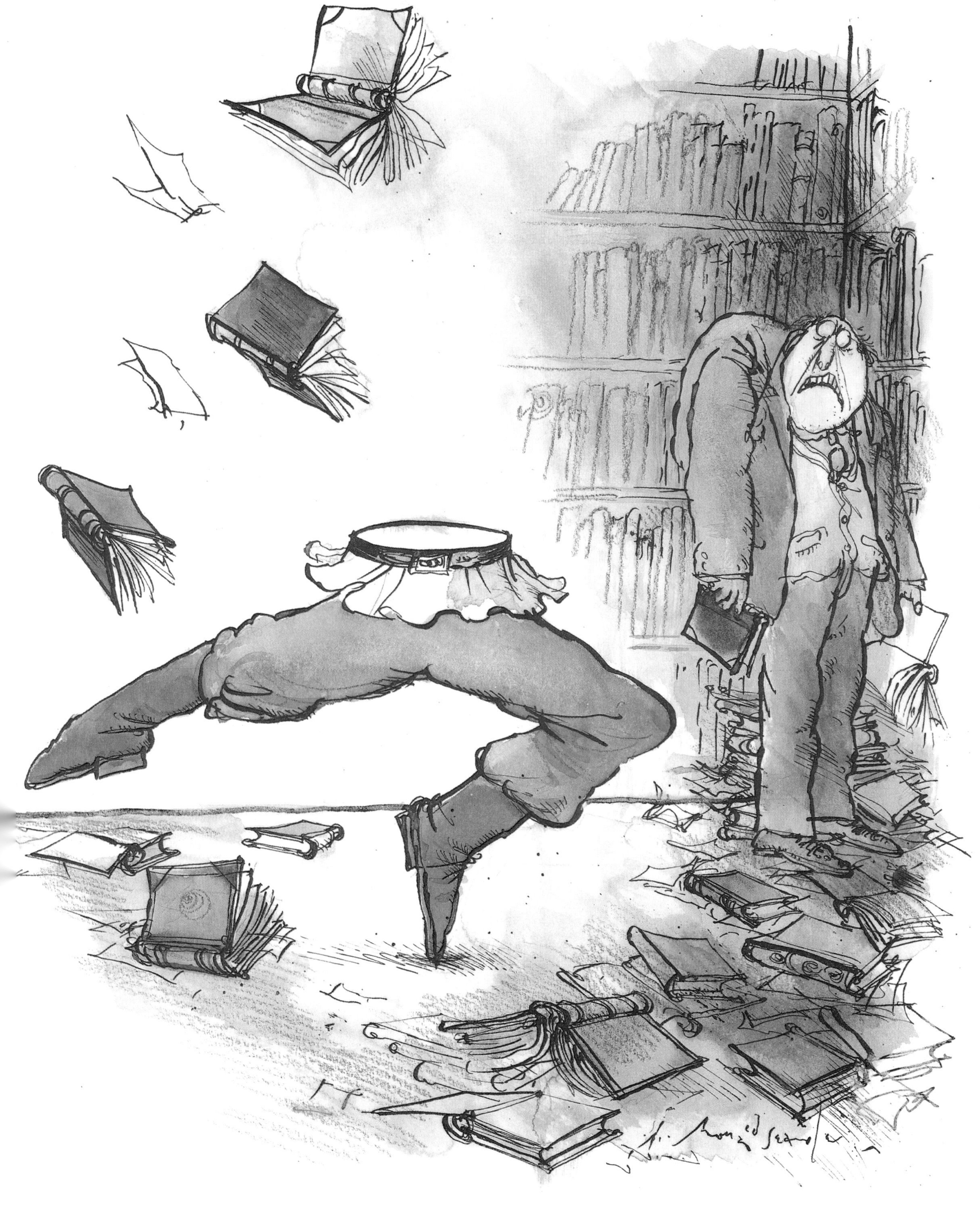

Blind-tooled

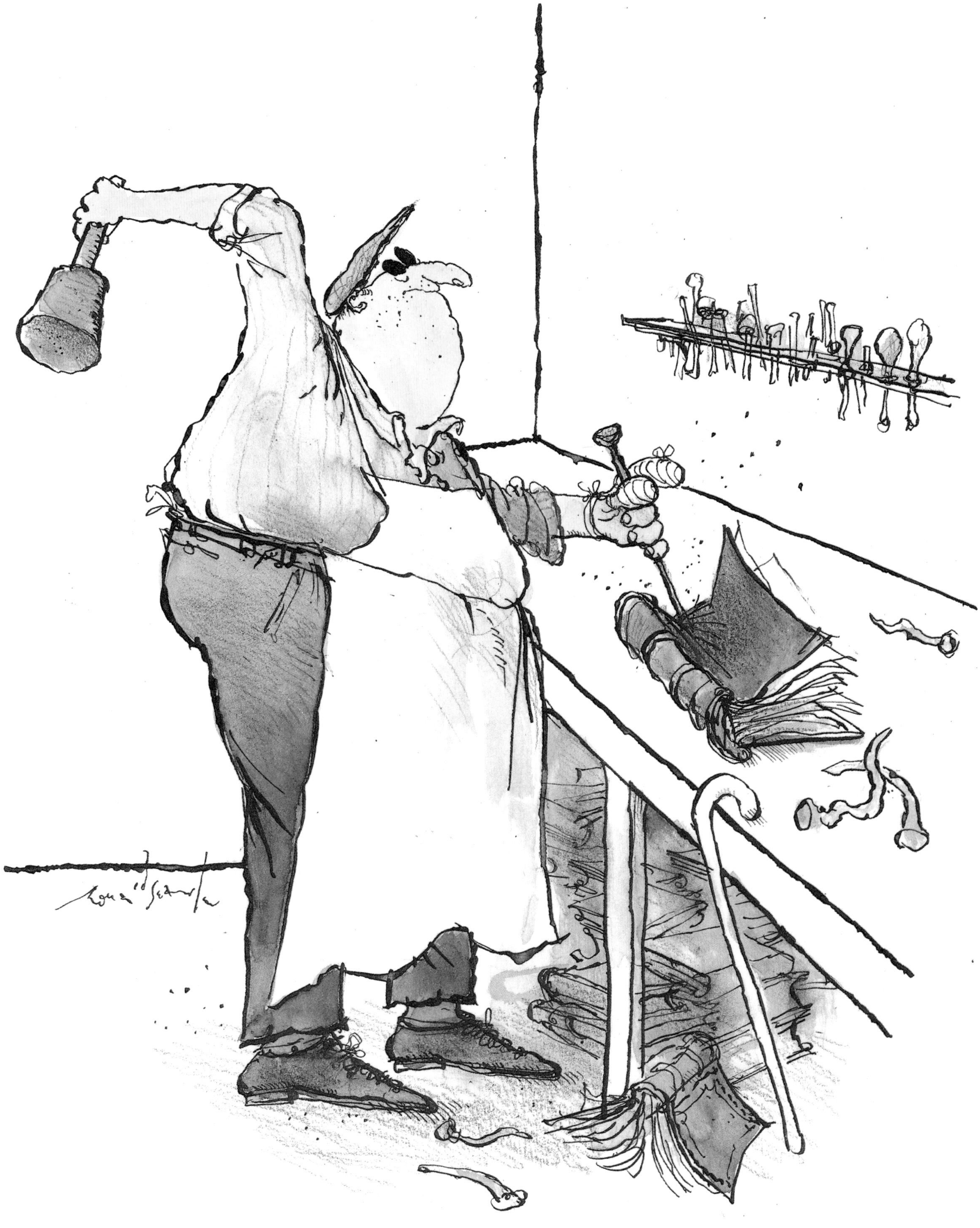

Neat underlining

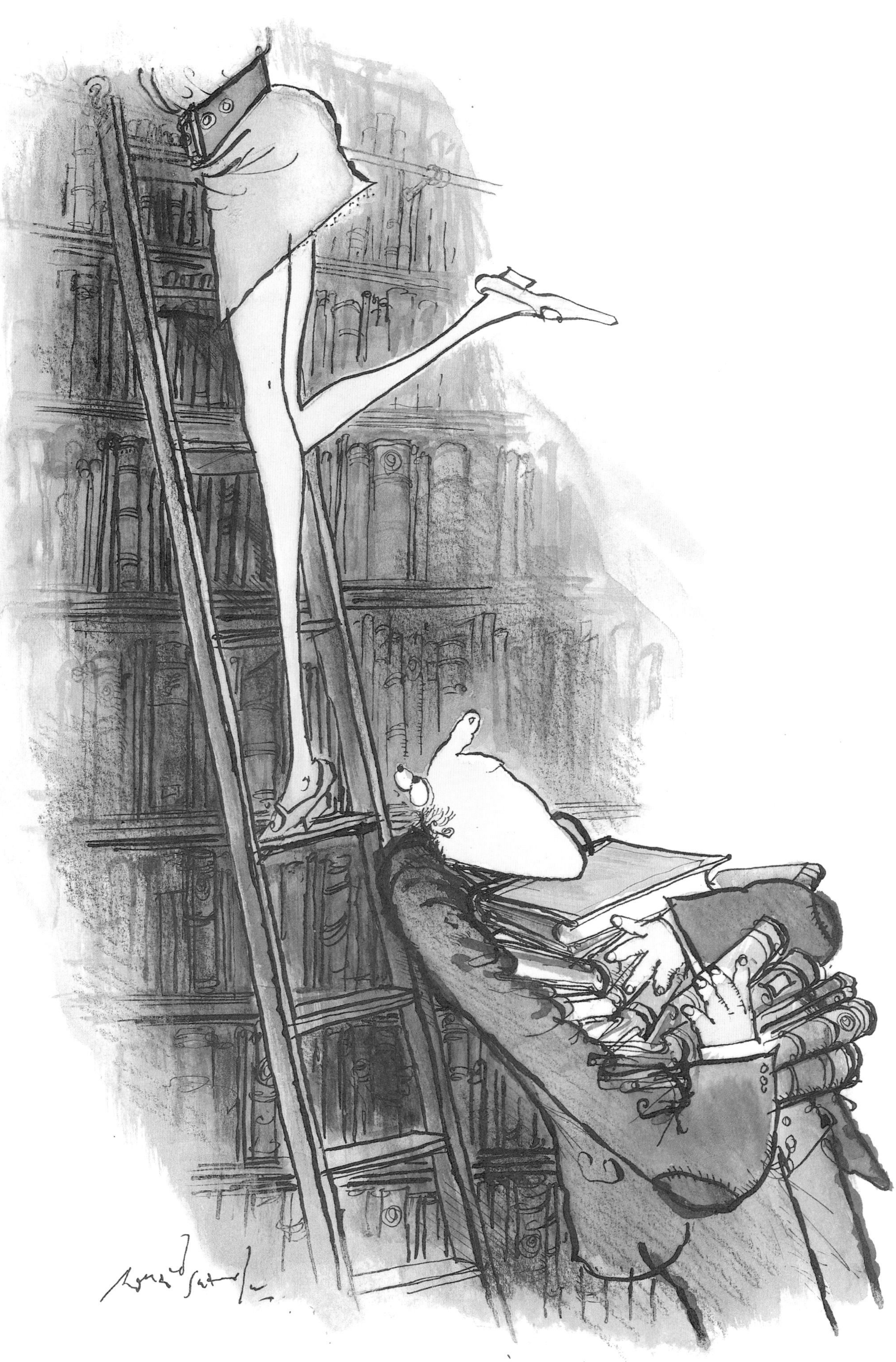

Slightly sprung

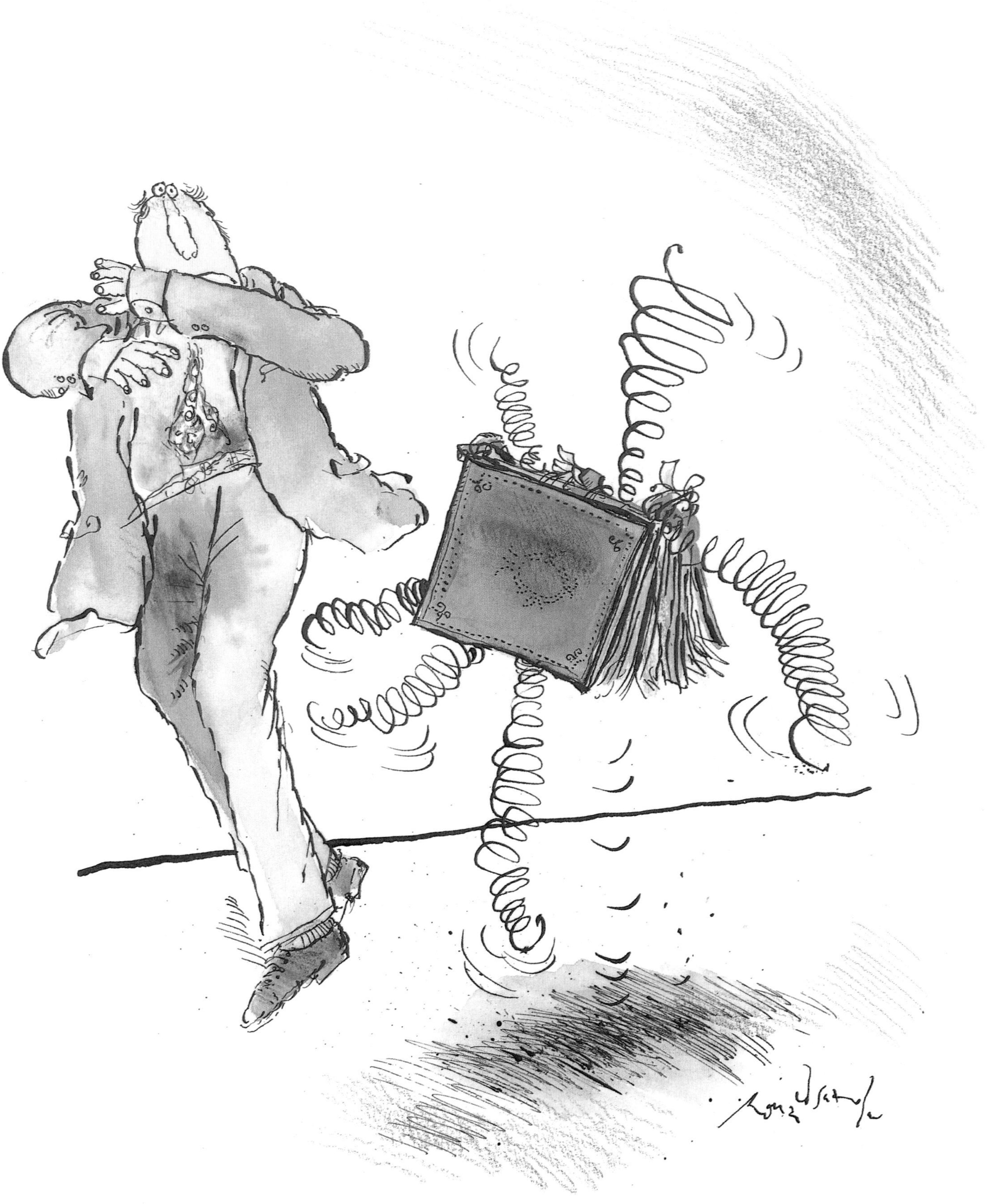

Tail-edge shaved

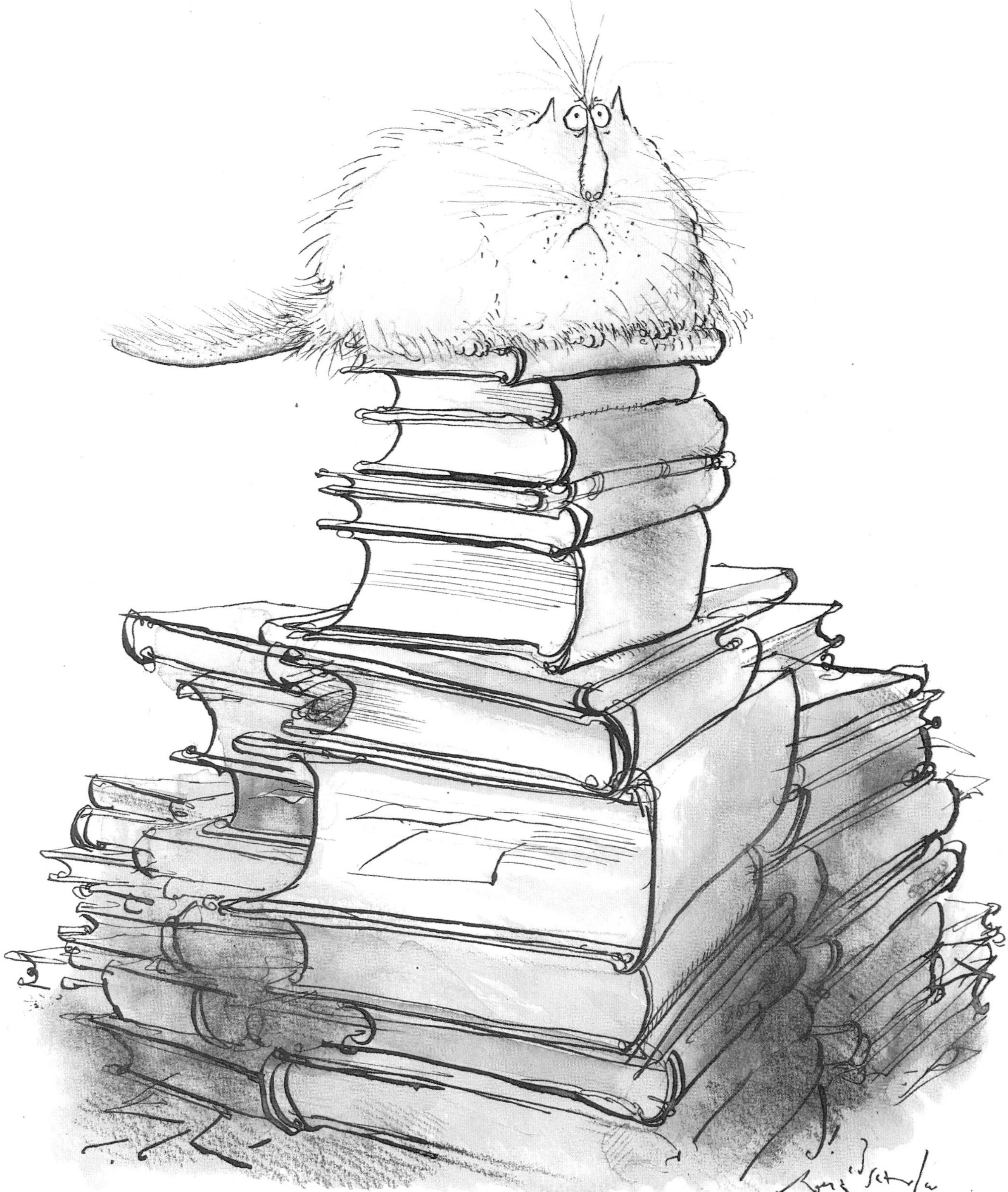

Some spots on back, but internally fresh

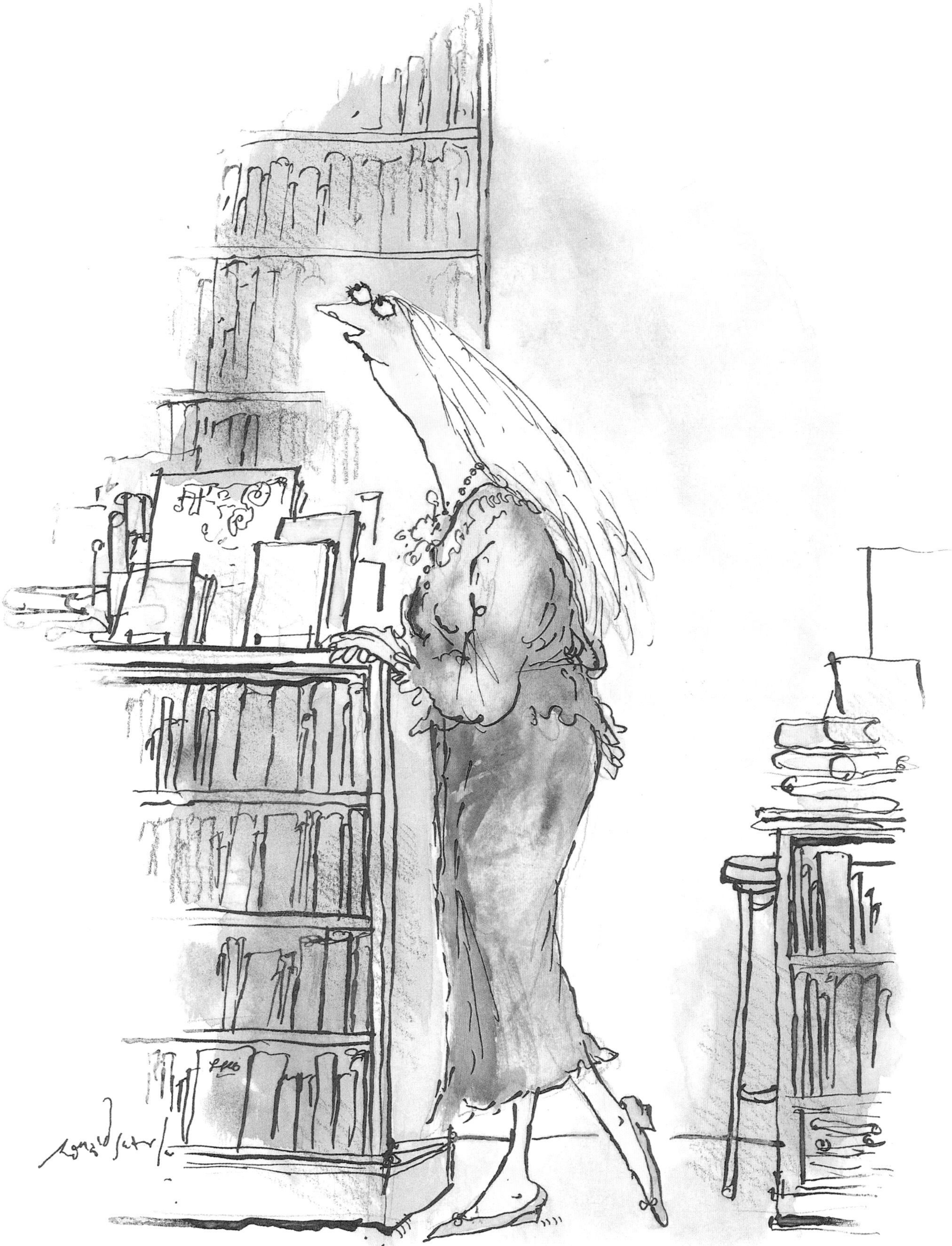

Outwardly cracking

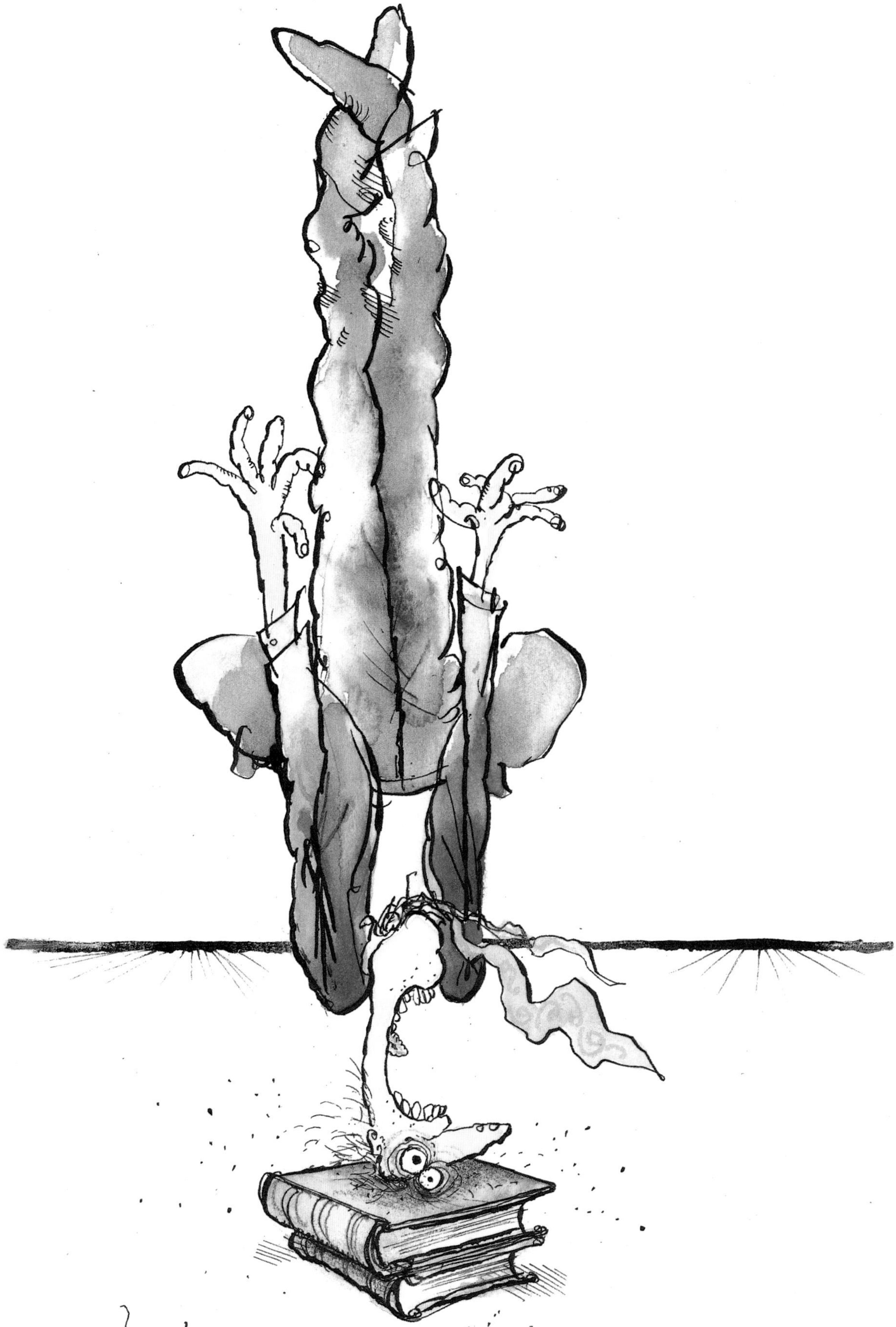

Some evidence of damp-staining

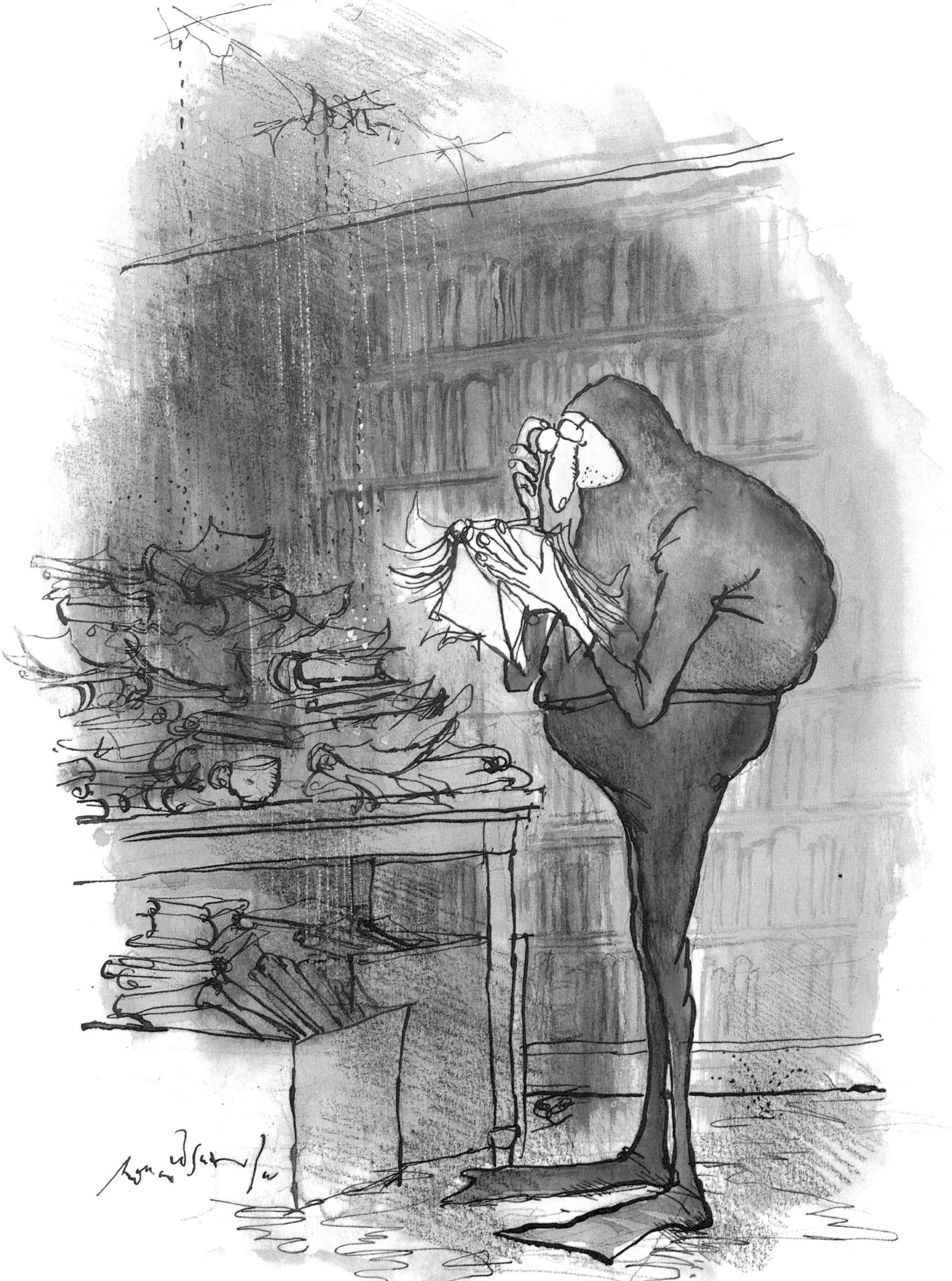

Foxed throughout

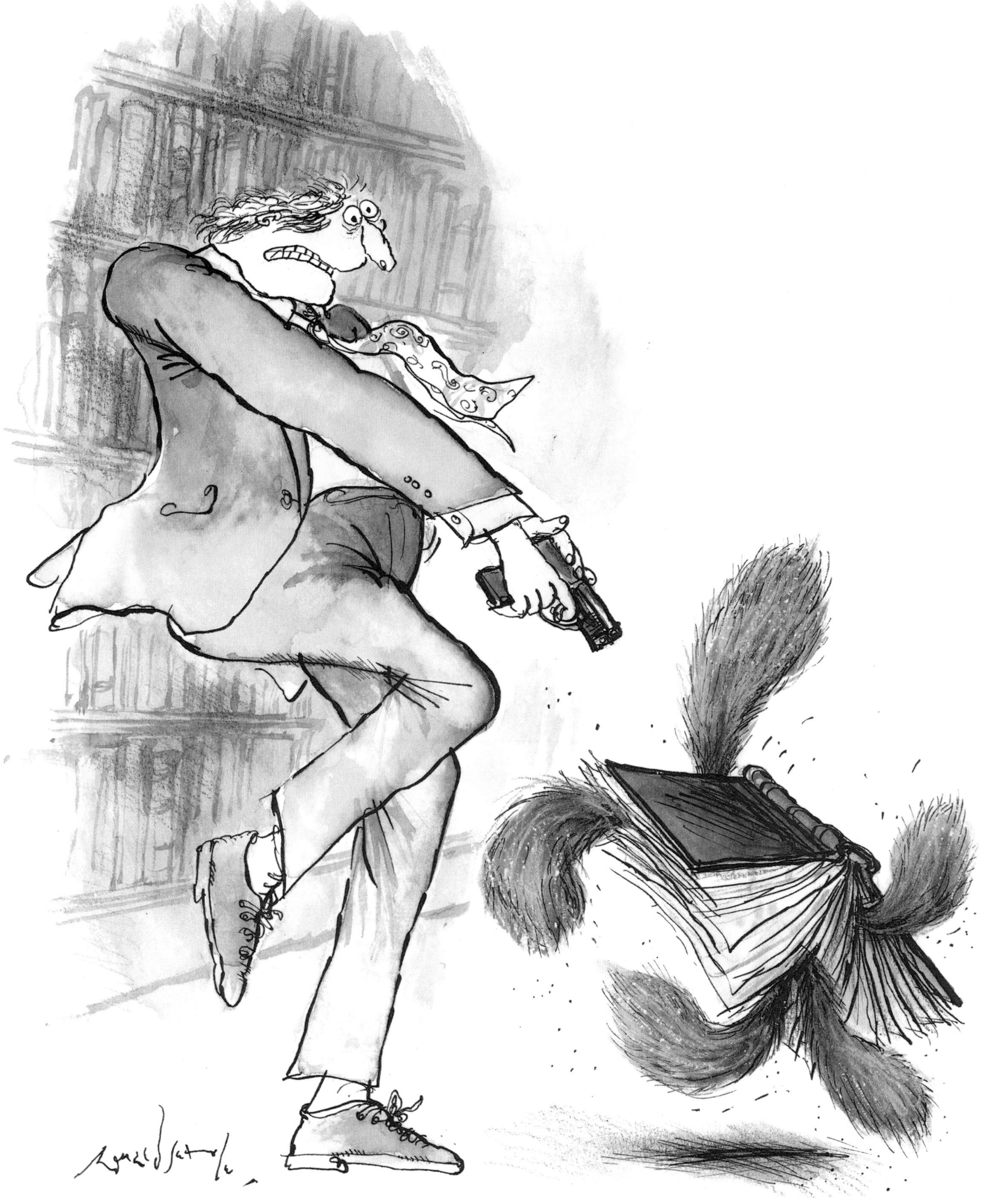

Disbound

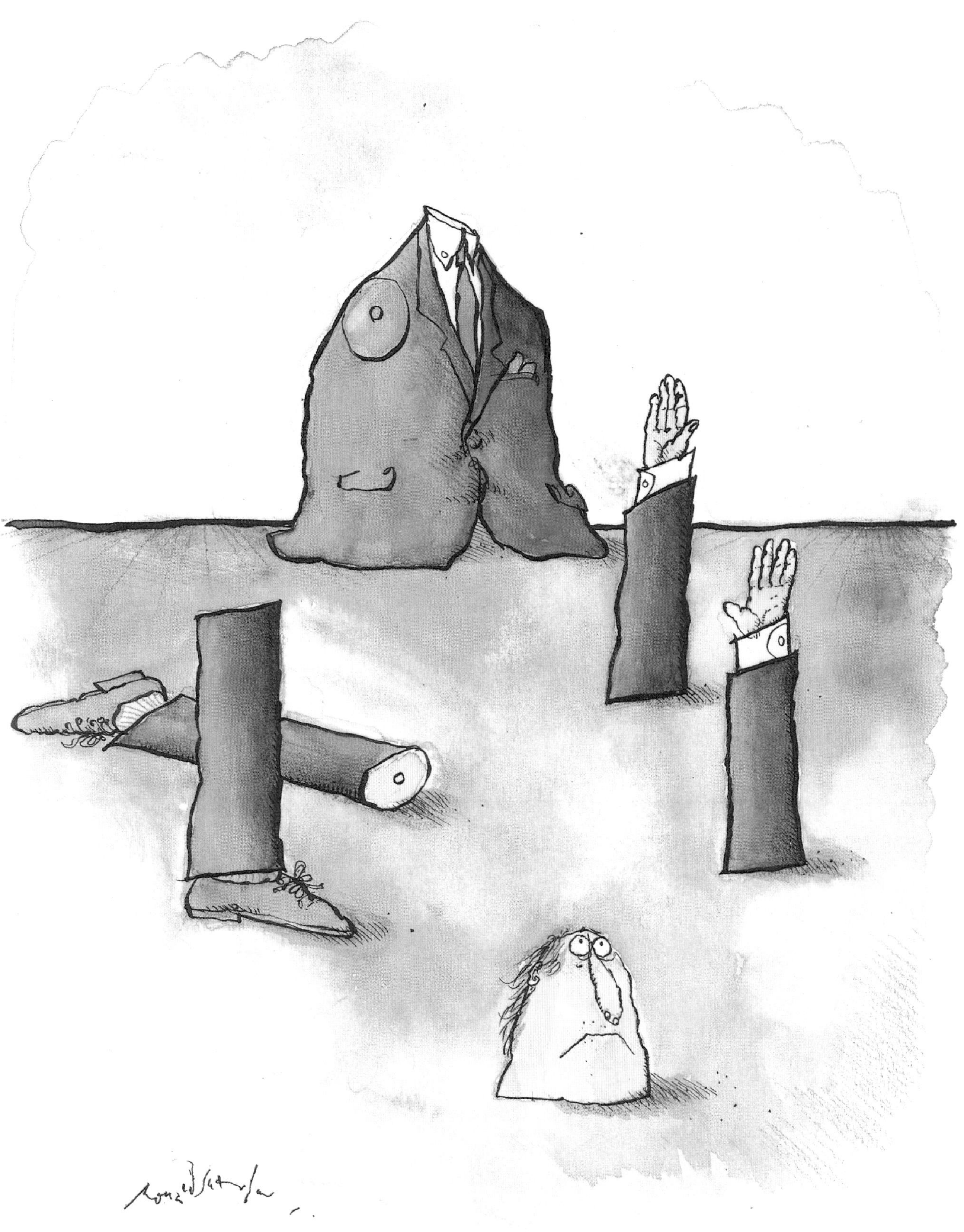

Old style calf

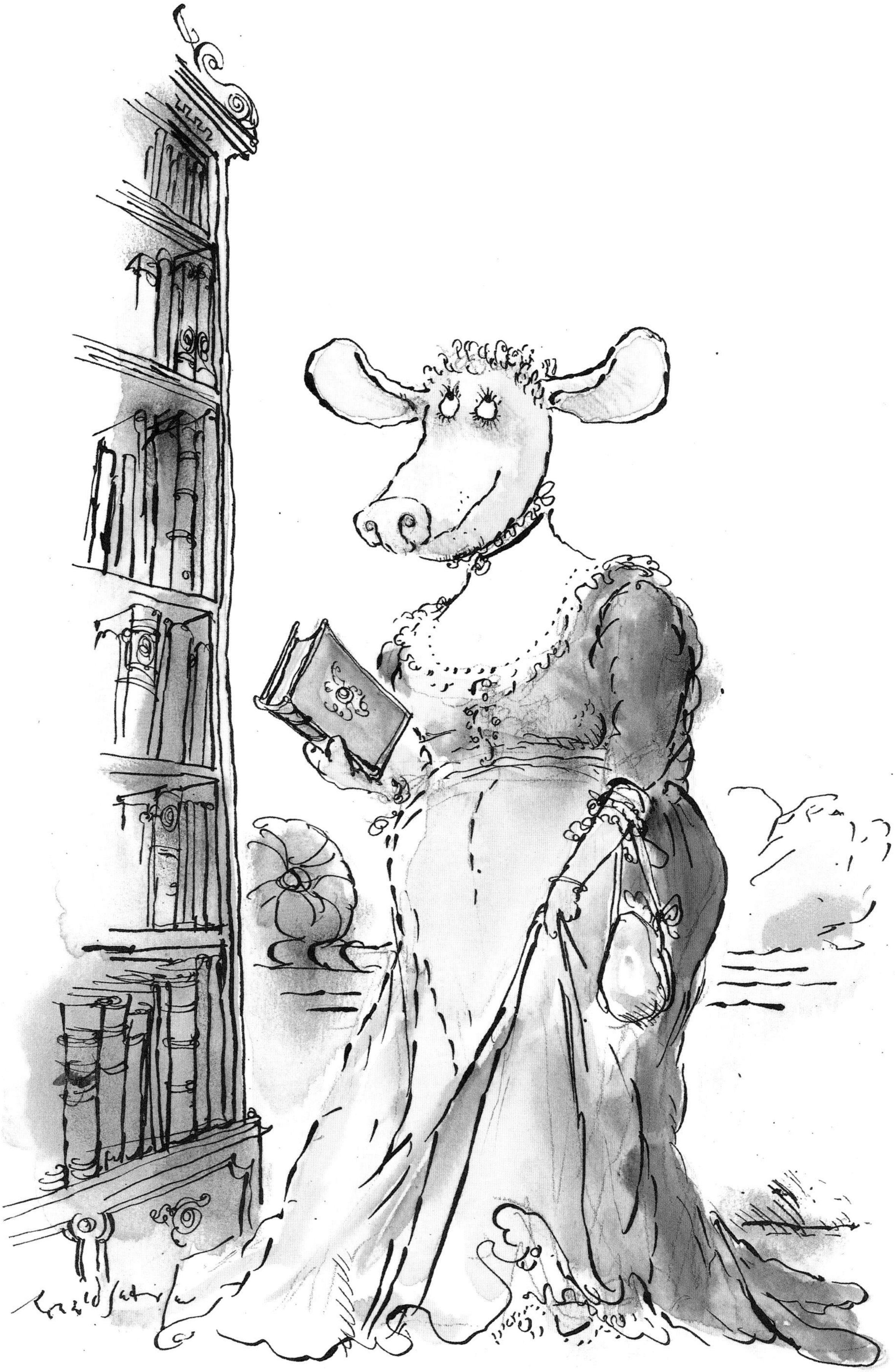

Numerous headpieces

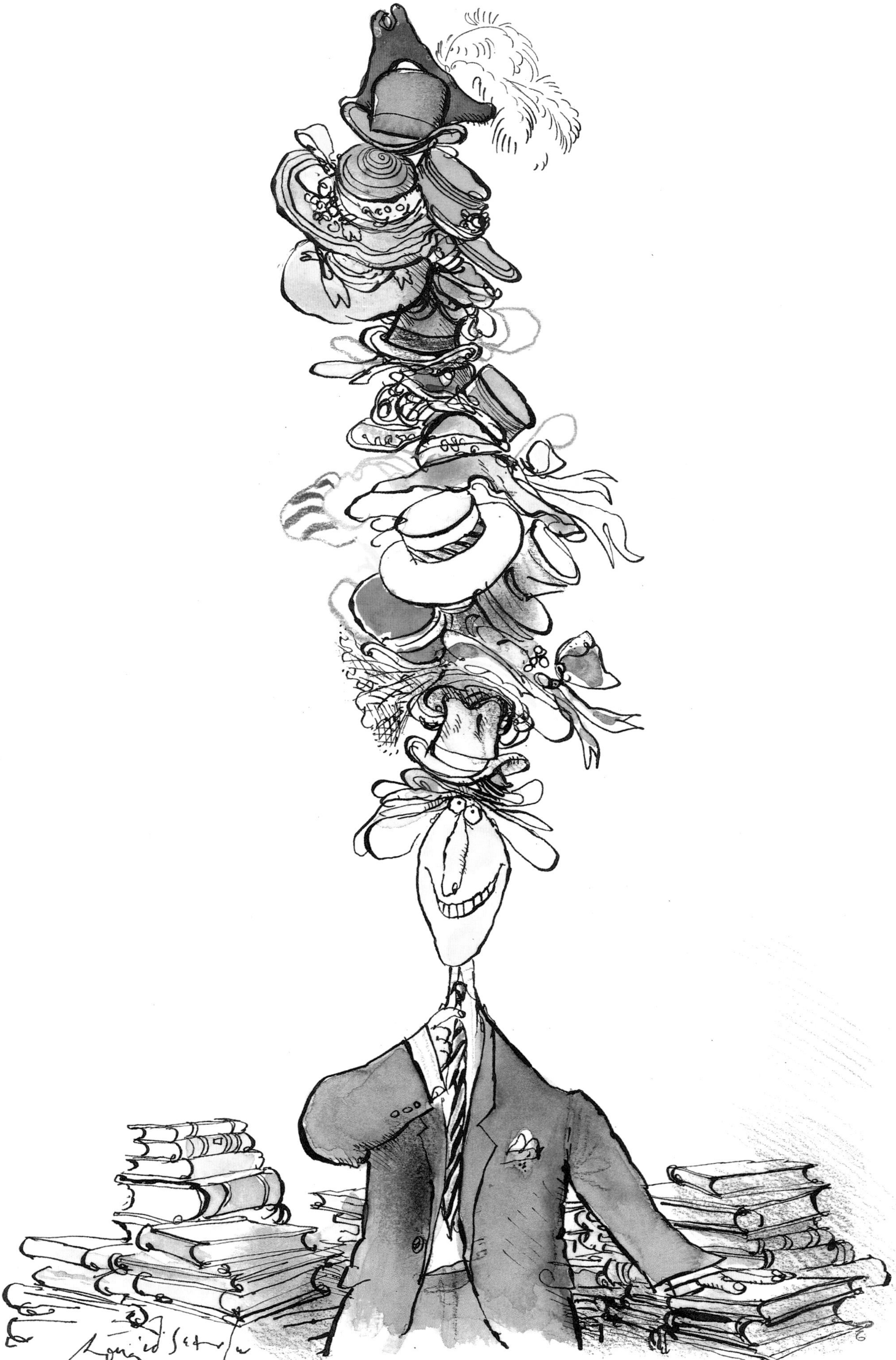

A pleasant set

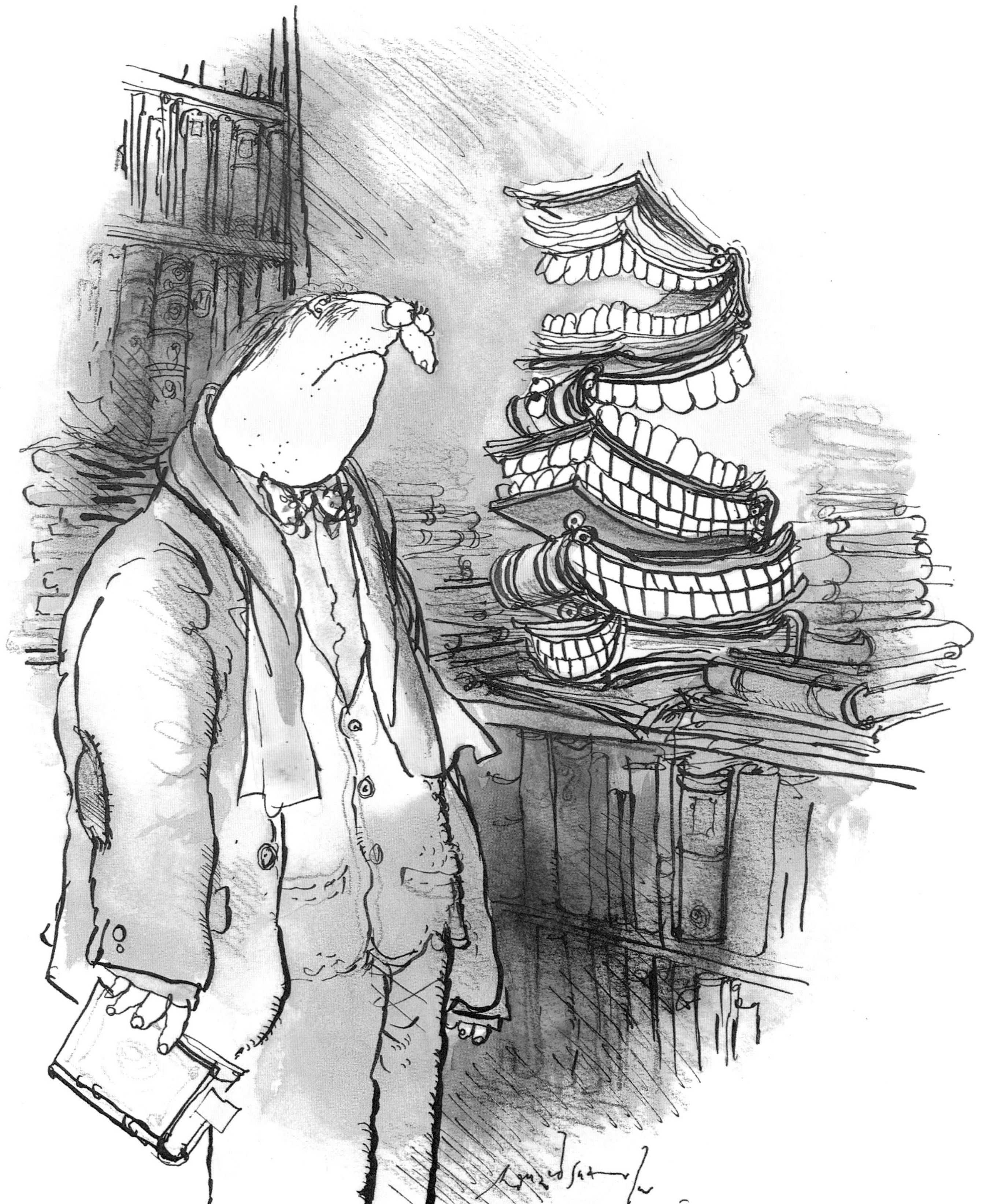

A little thumbed, otherwise an attractive copy

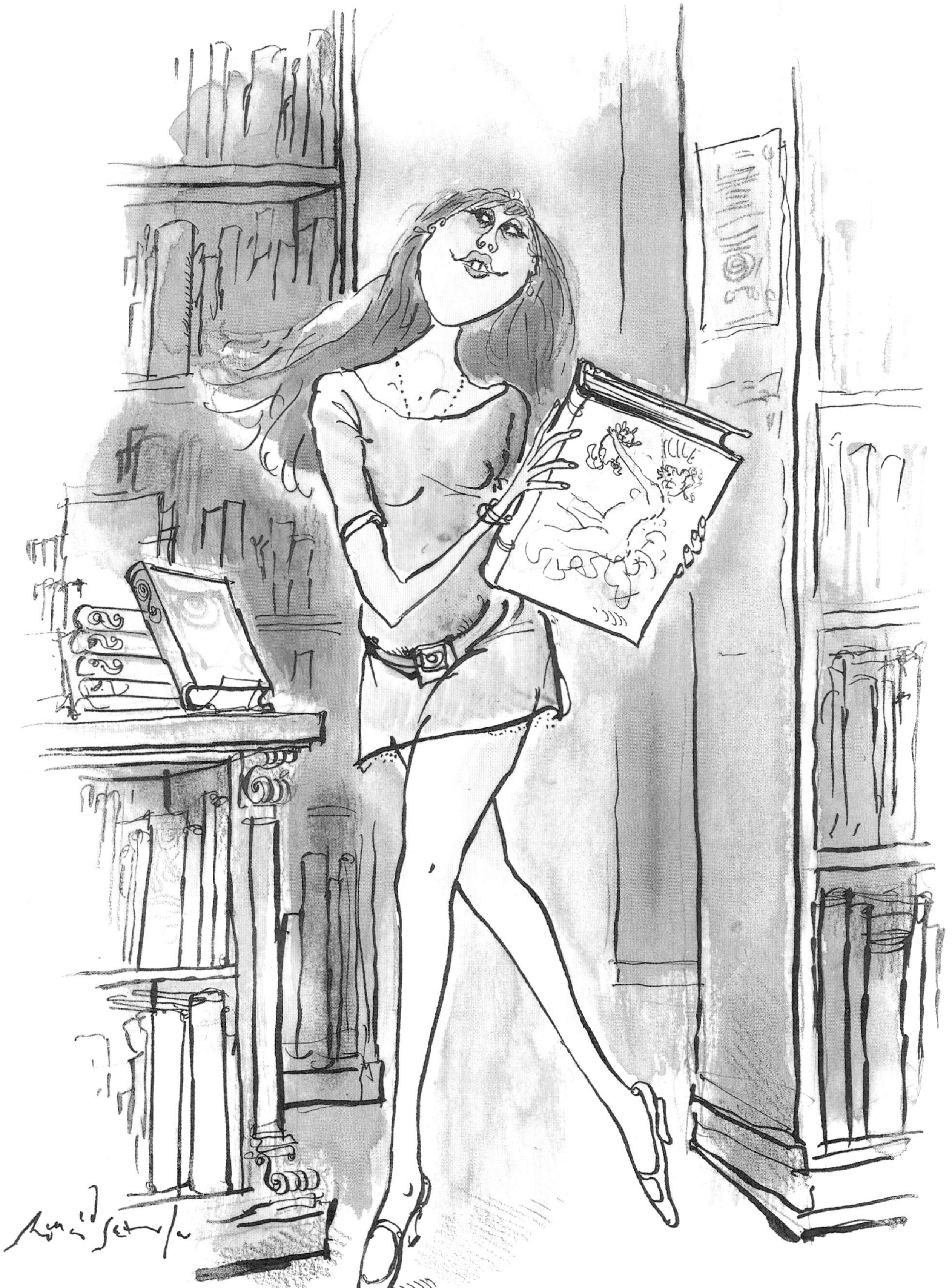

Some worming of the epoch

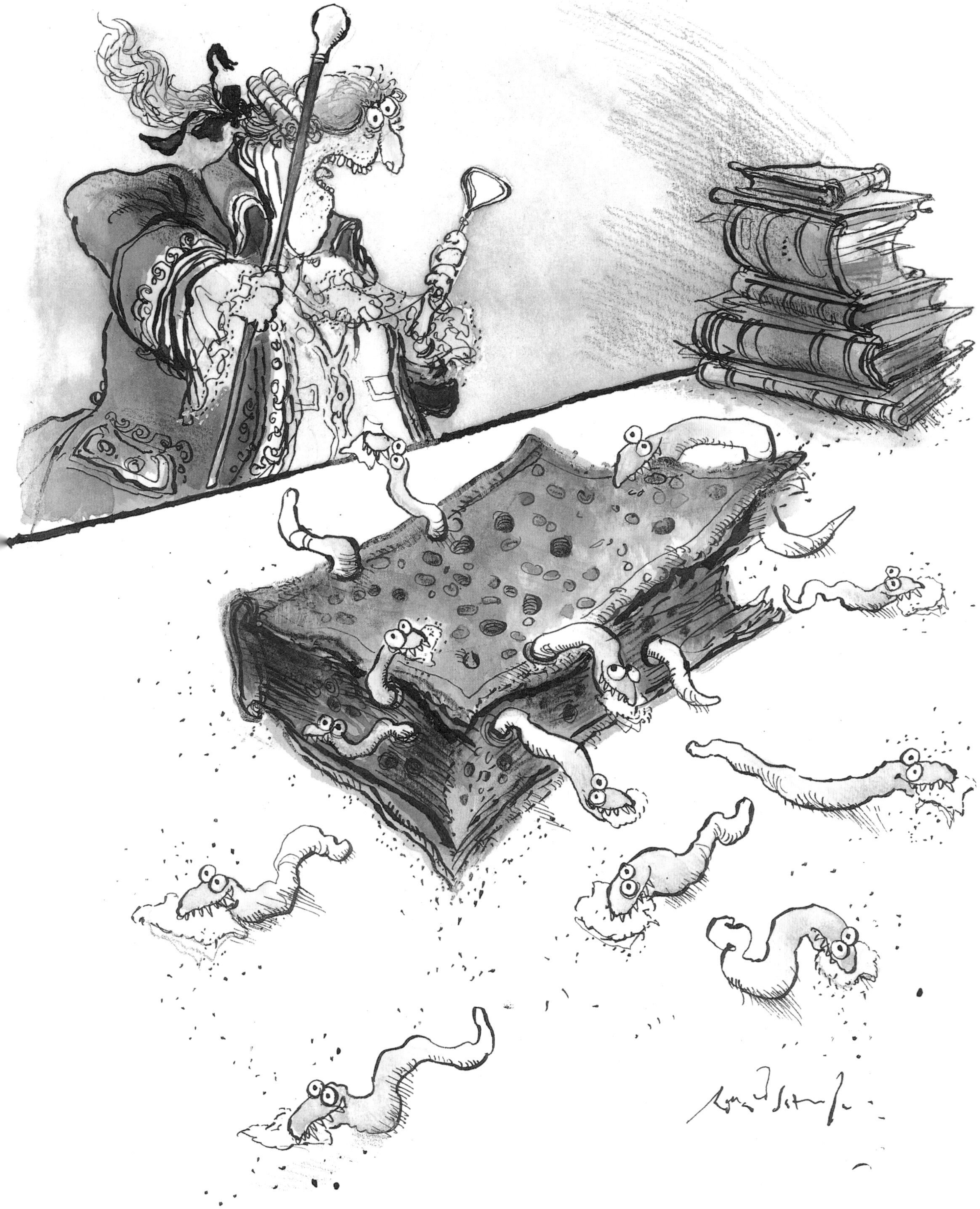

Stitching a little loose

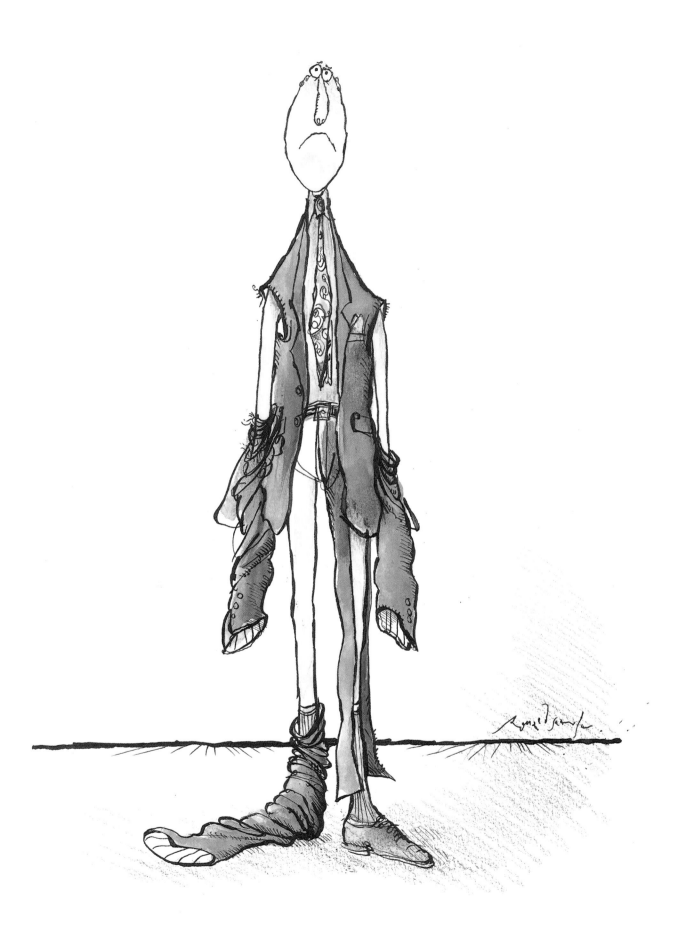

Unwashed, with only slight marginal soiling

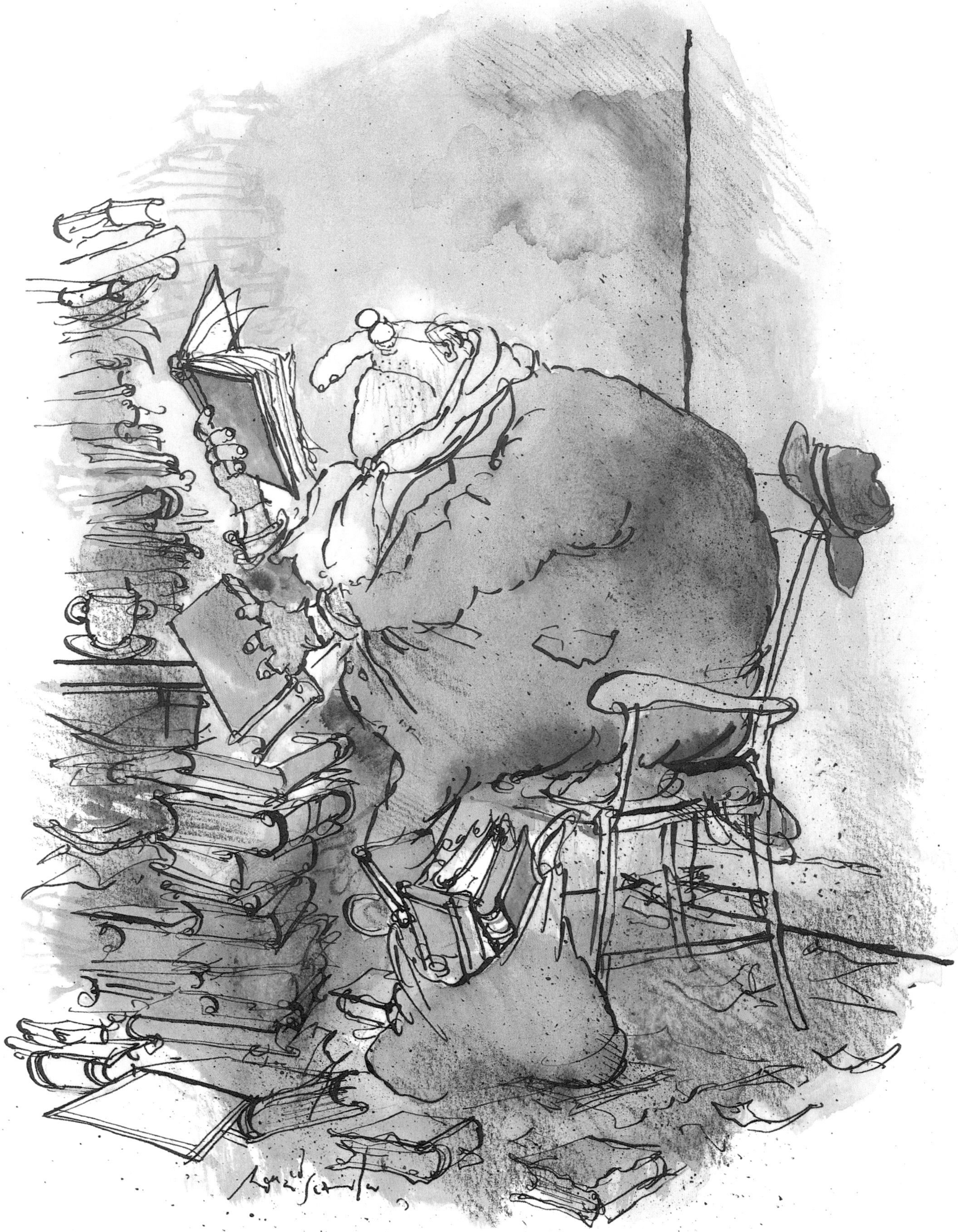

Running title

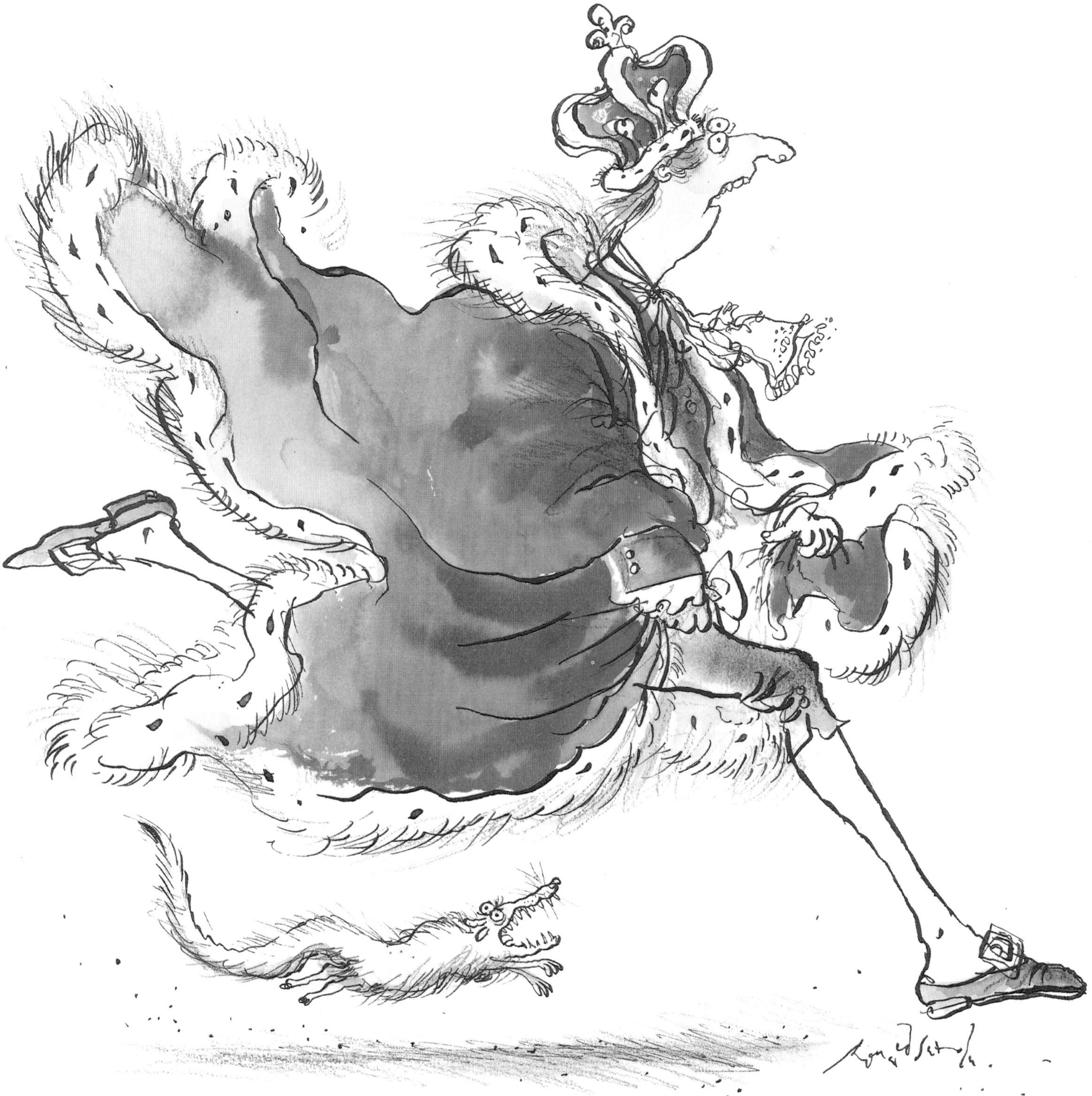

Slight splitting of paste-downs

Spine defective

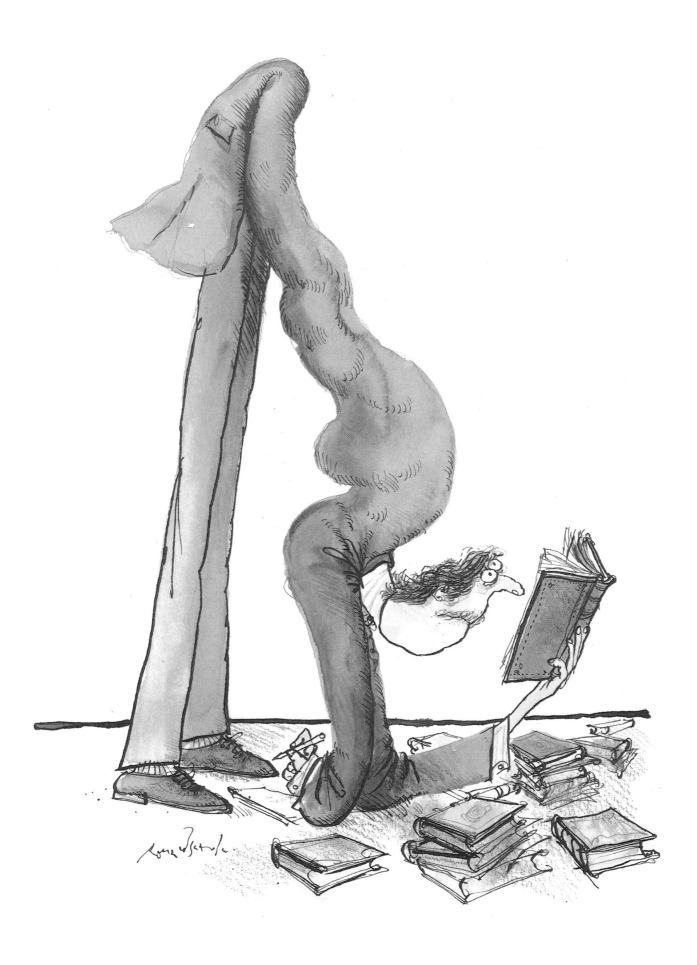

Numerous critical marginal notes in a contemporary hand

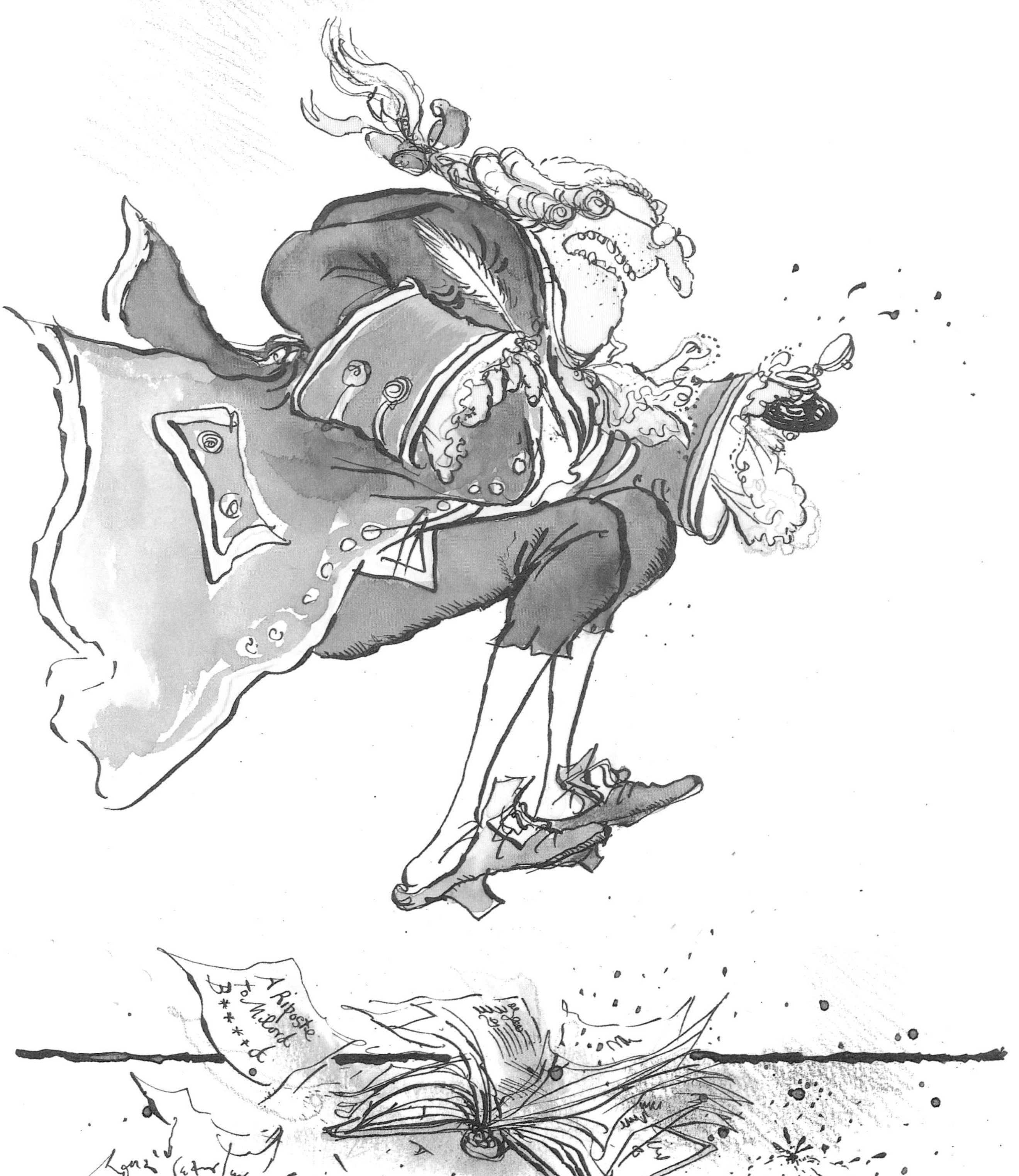
A Riposte
to Milord
B****d

Dented at head

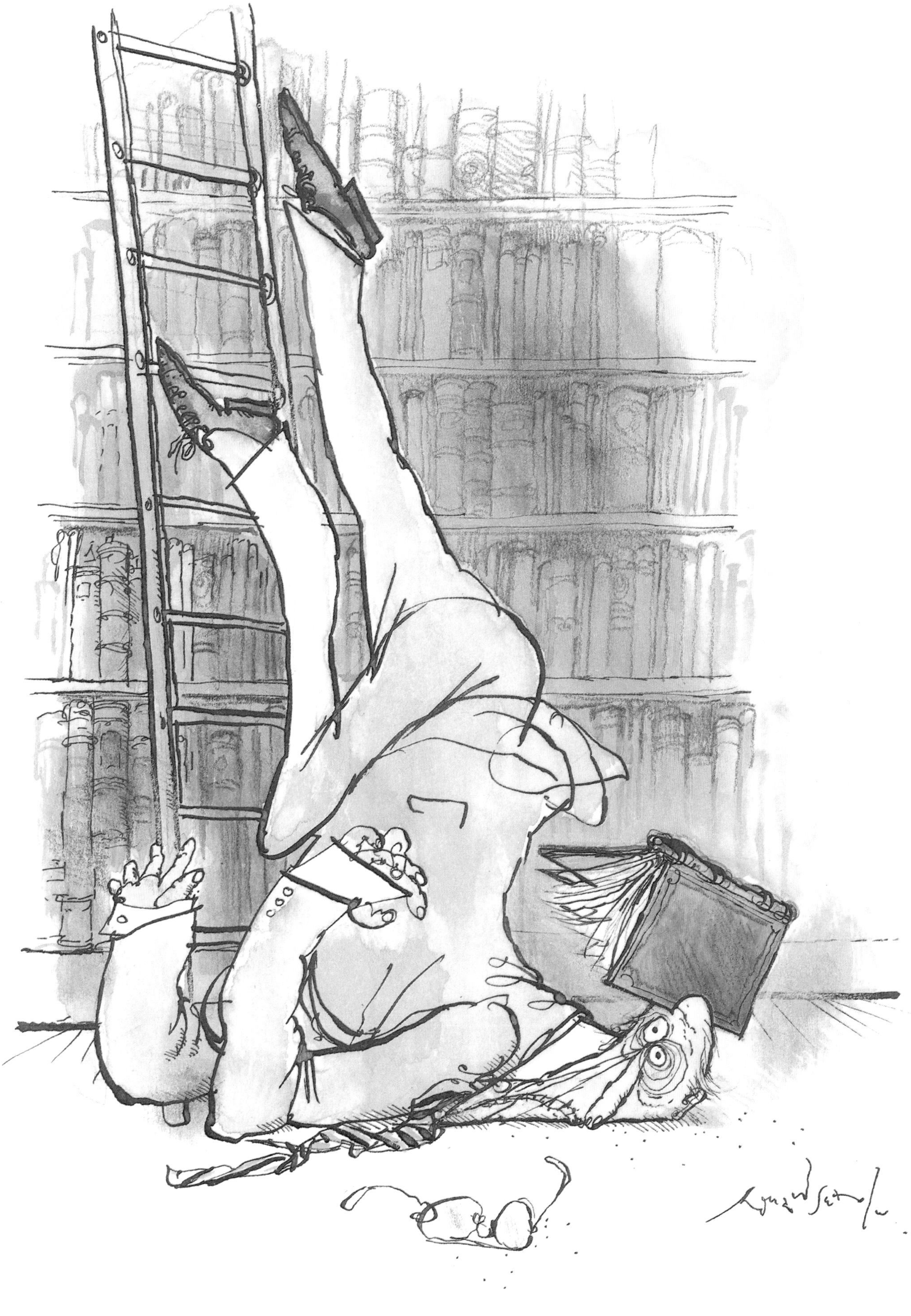

Some graffiti of the period

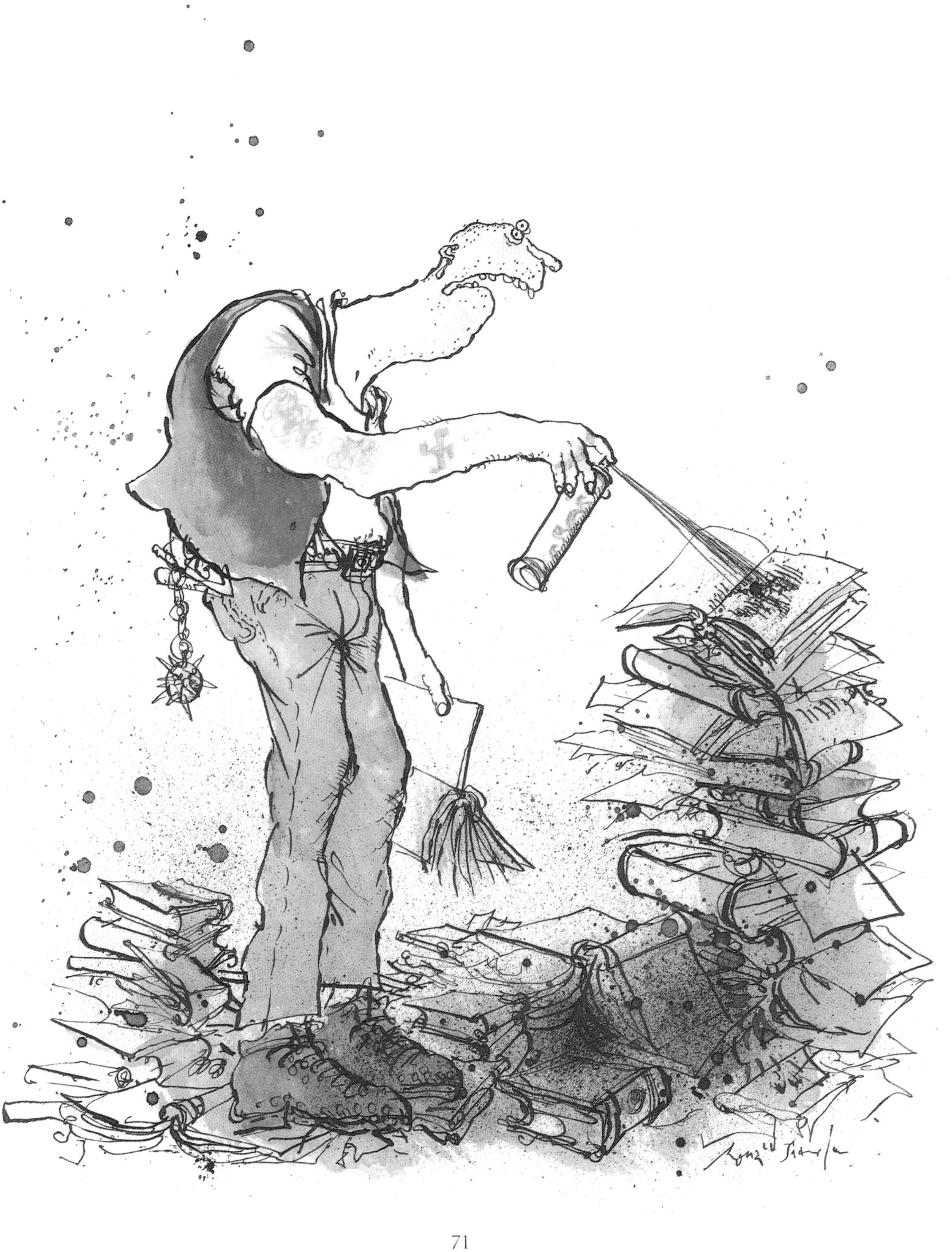

The Maggs—de Nobele—Quaritch—Elte—
Parikian—Wormser—Pedersen—Magee—
Grant copy. Missing leaf supplied in
facsimile.

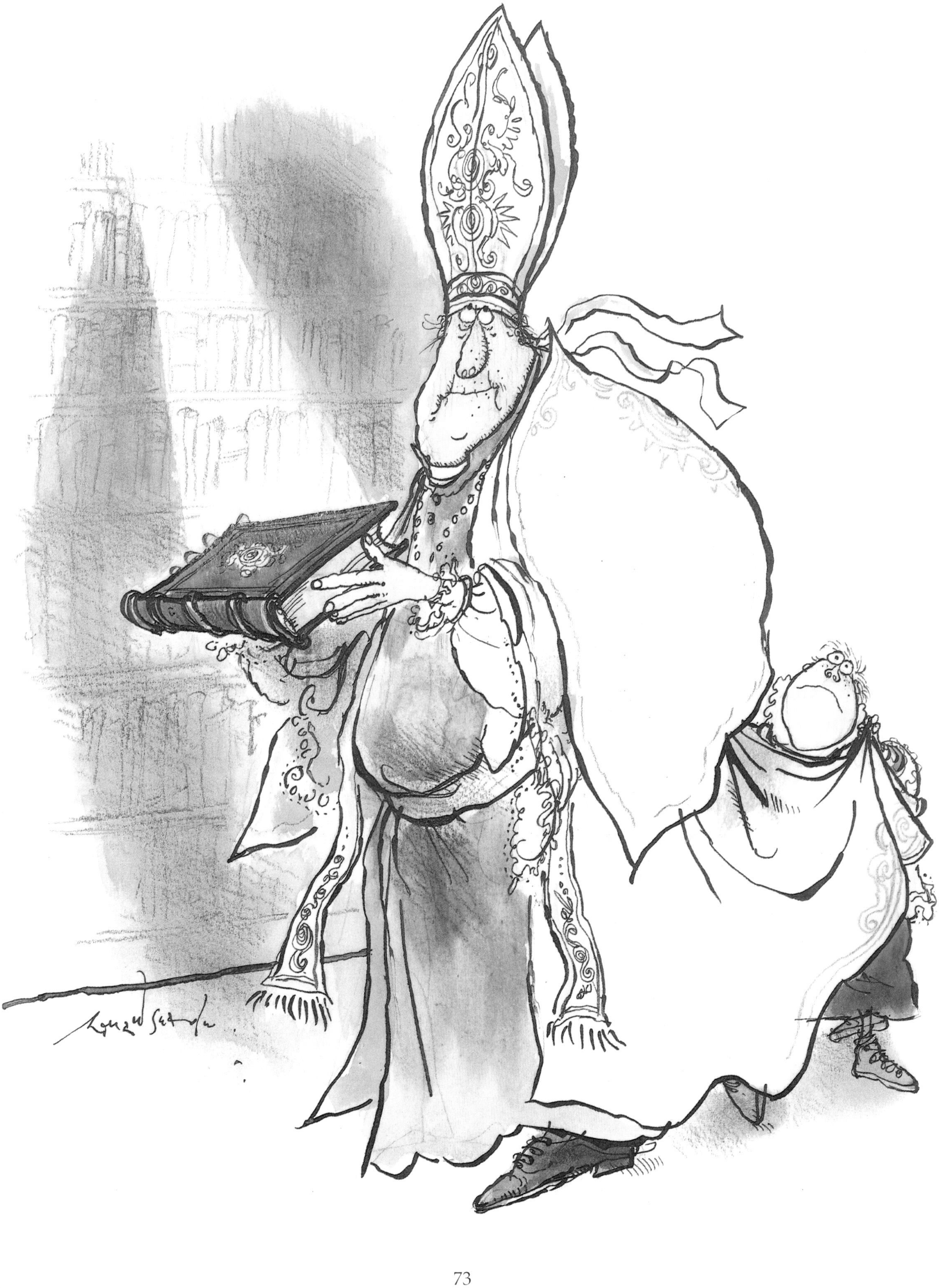

Generally a little loose

Fabric tie removed

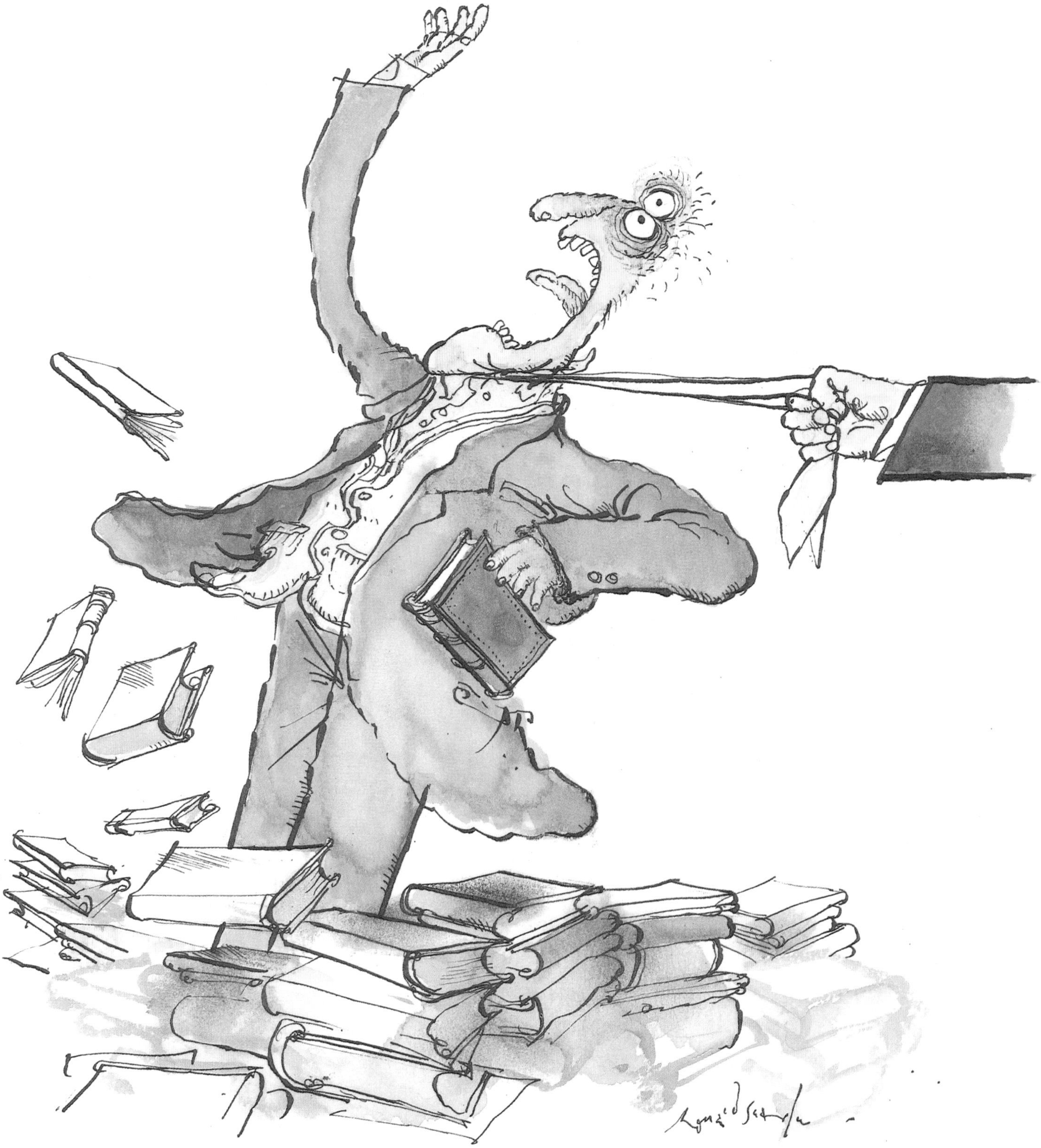

Lovingly thumbed by former owner

Early manuscript notes

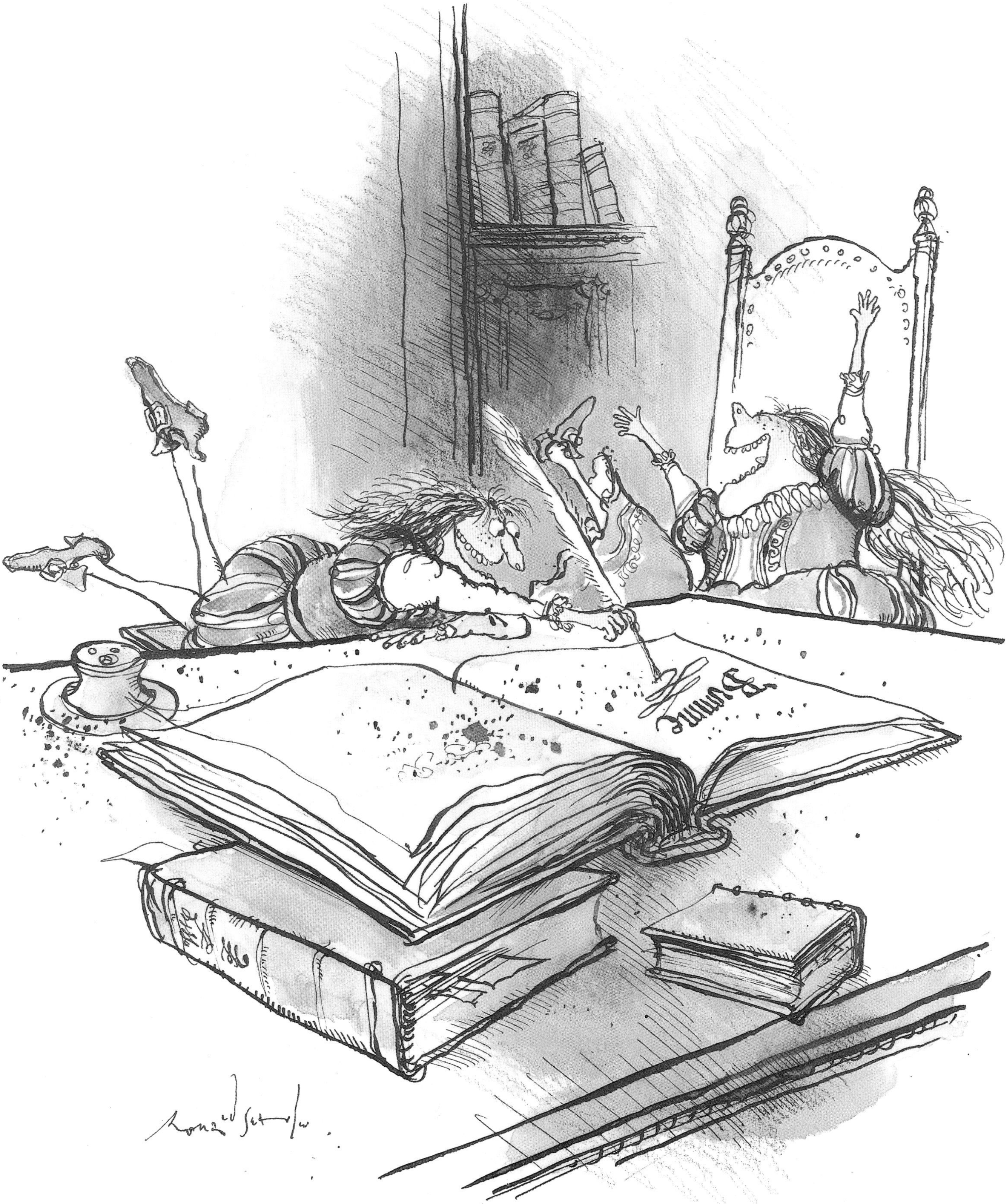

Pseudo–Morocco

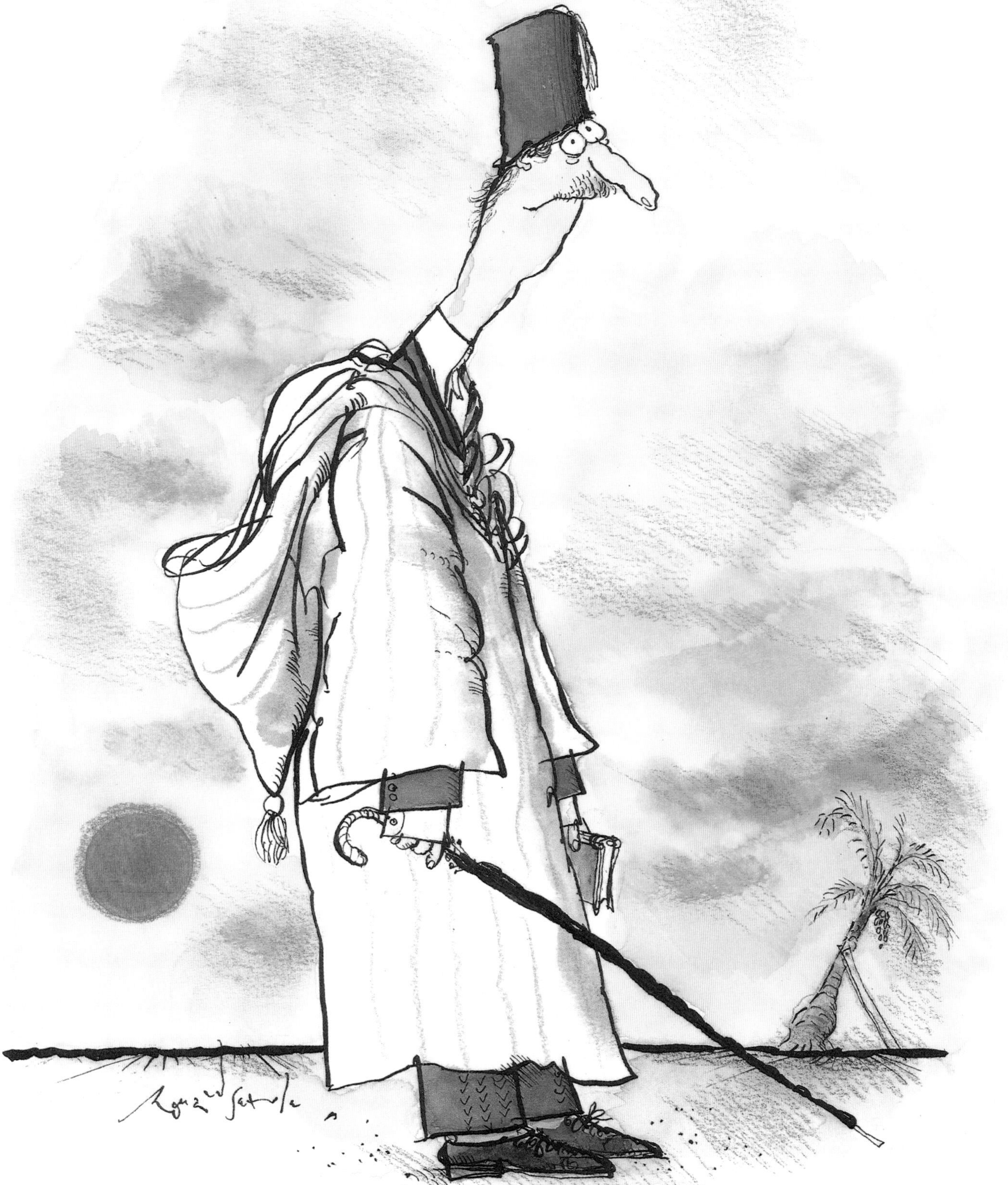

A nice bright set

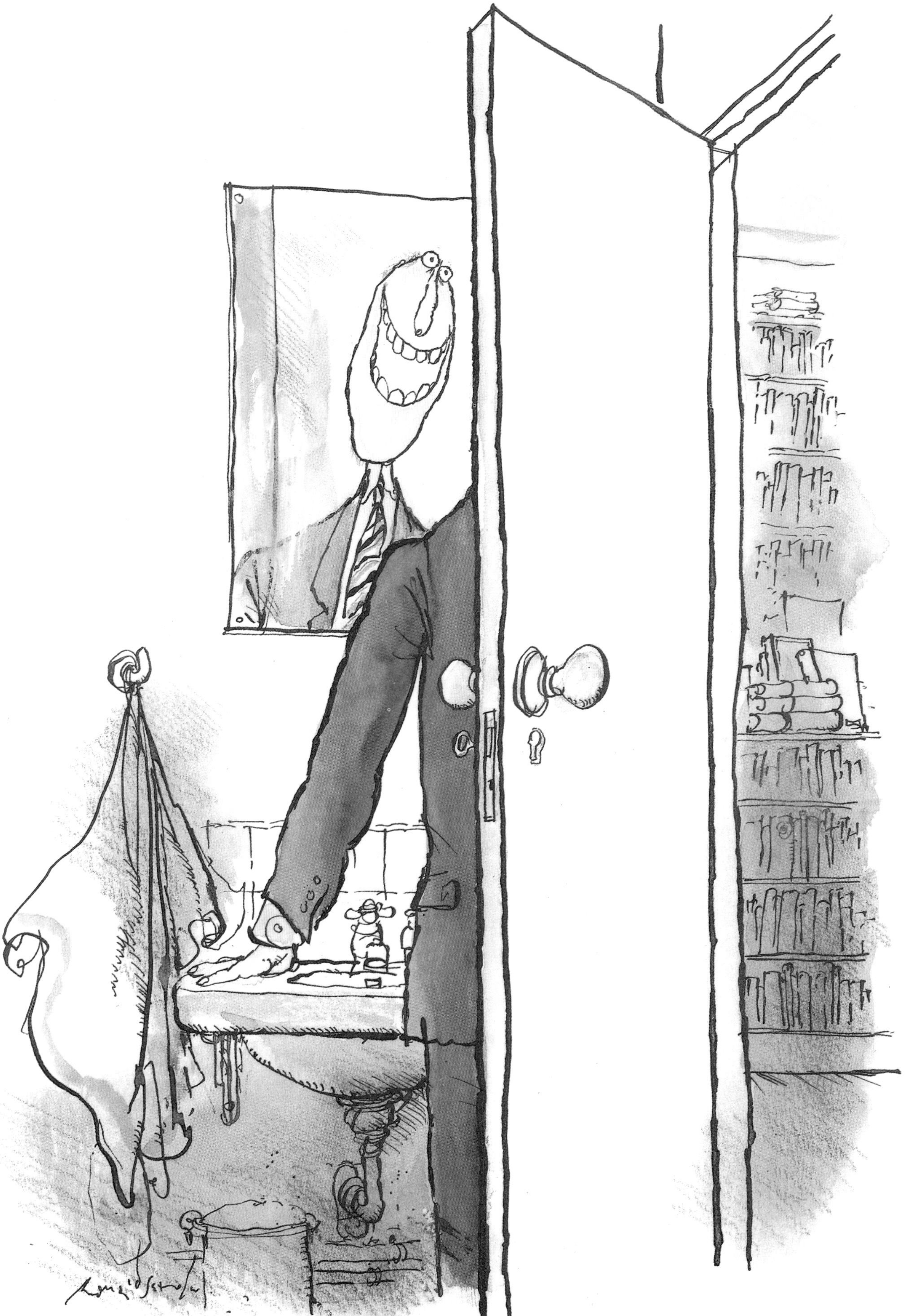

Signature sprung

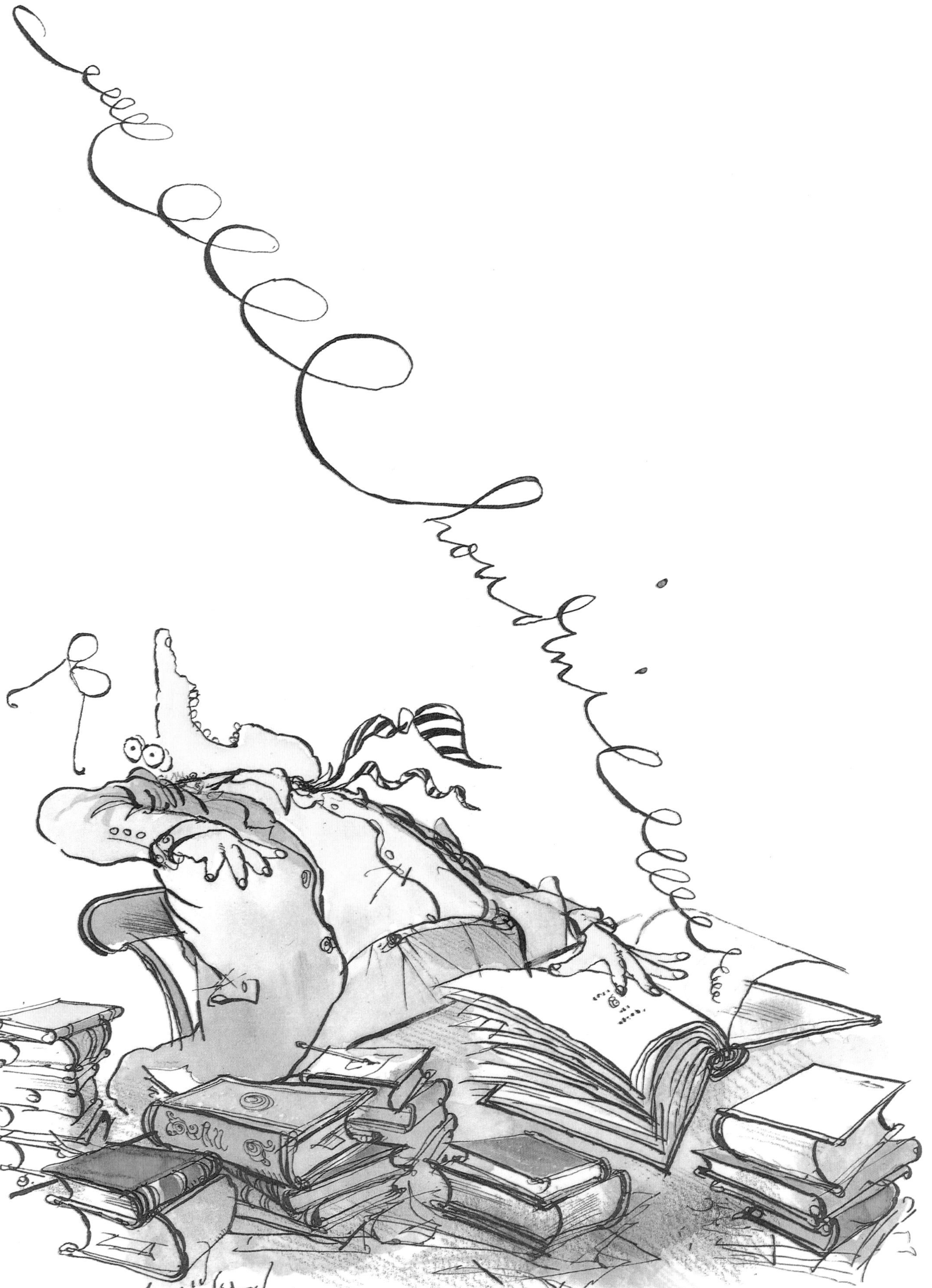

Bound together in a single volume

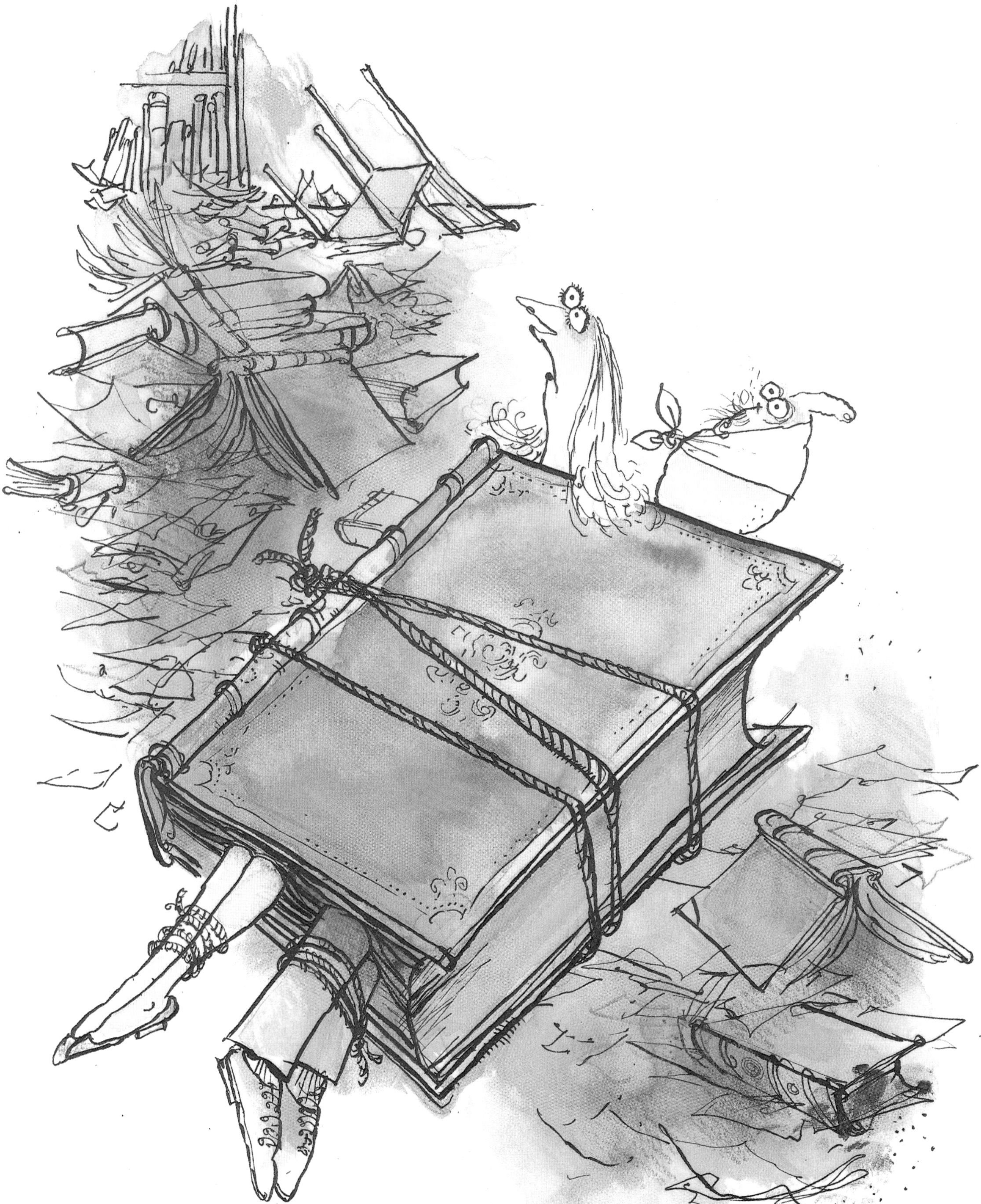

Coloured frontispiece present

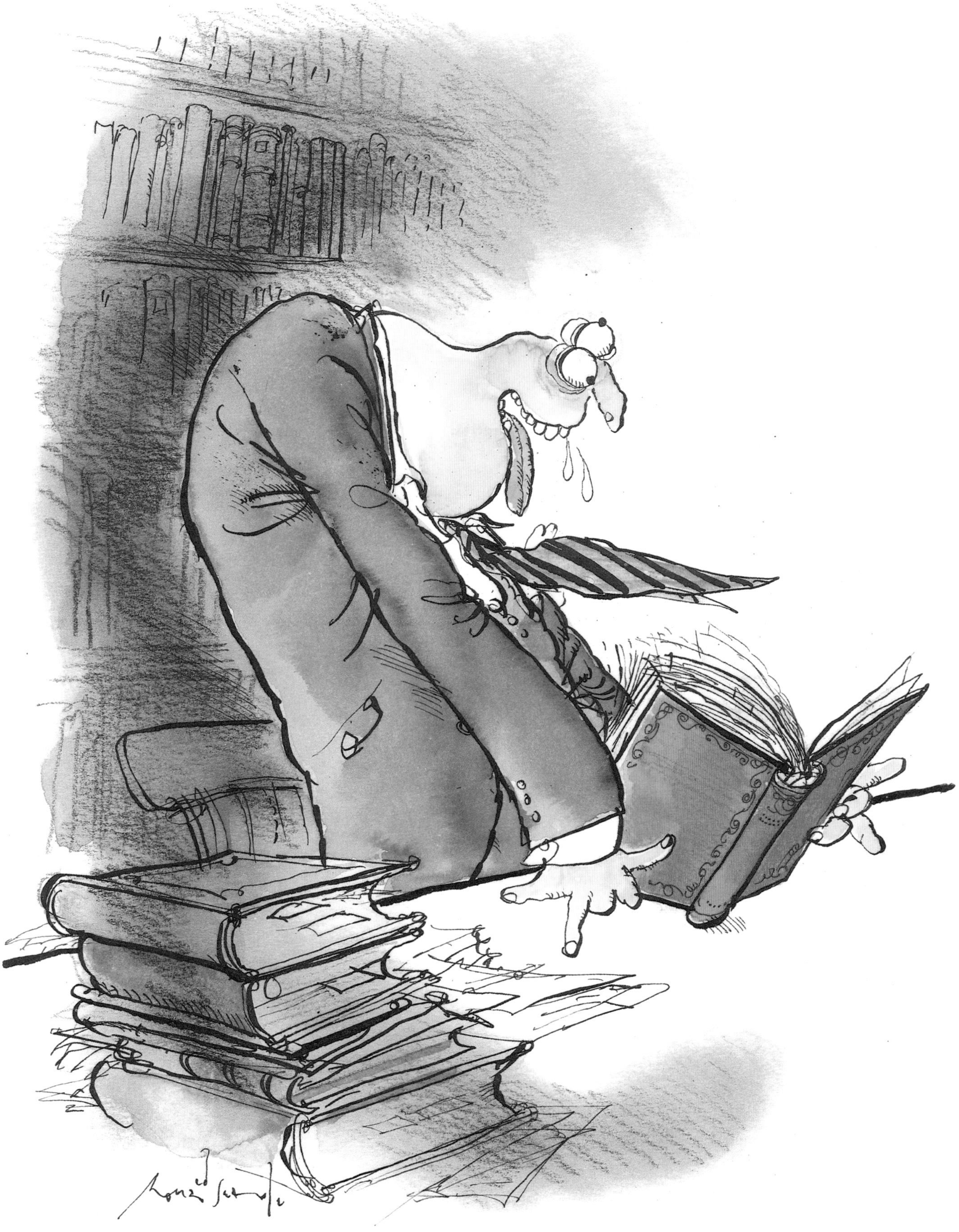

£35 until December 31st, £50 thereafter

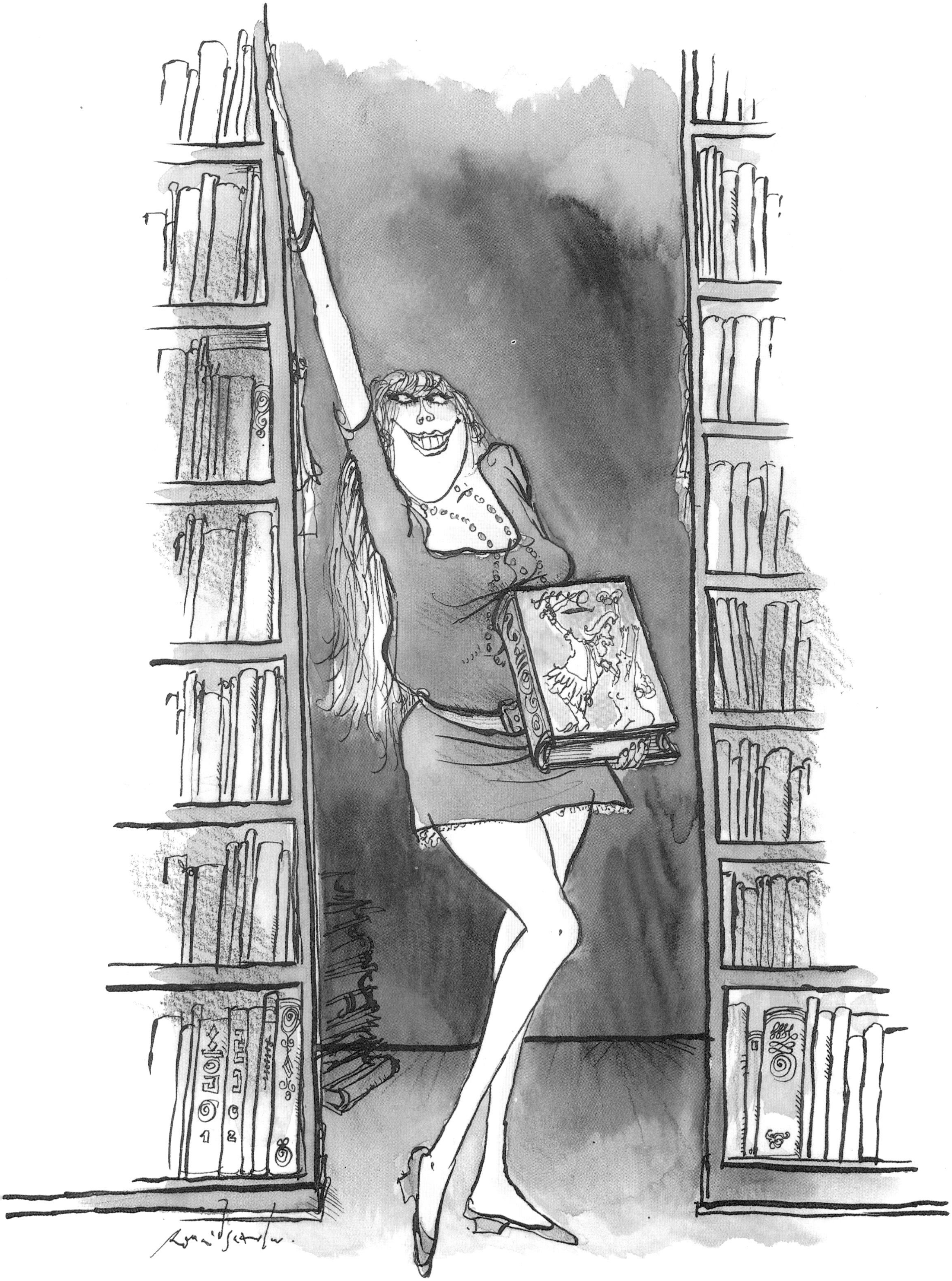

Cracked, but holding

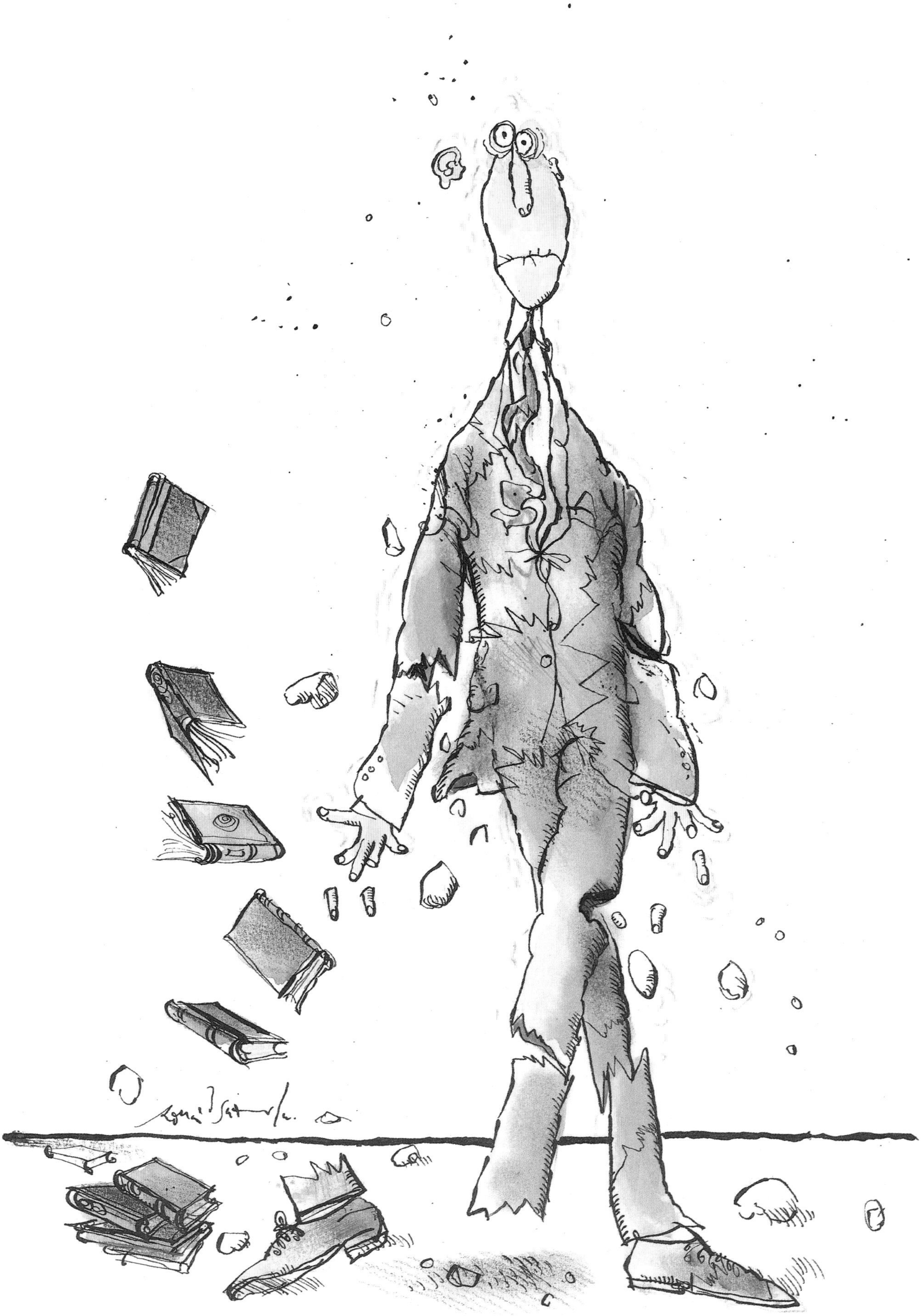

One corner barked

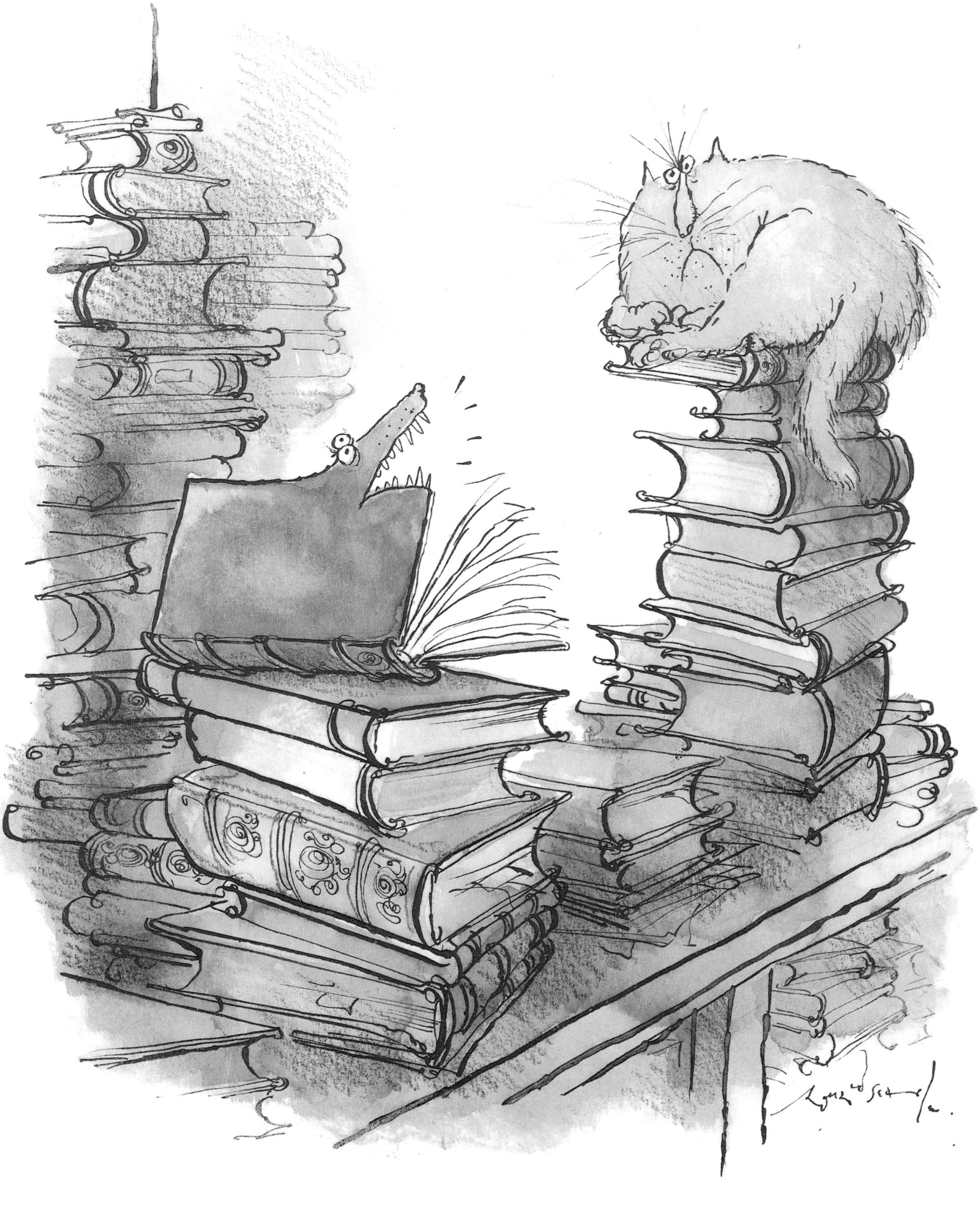

Ingeniously restored

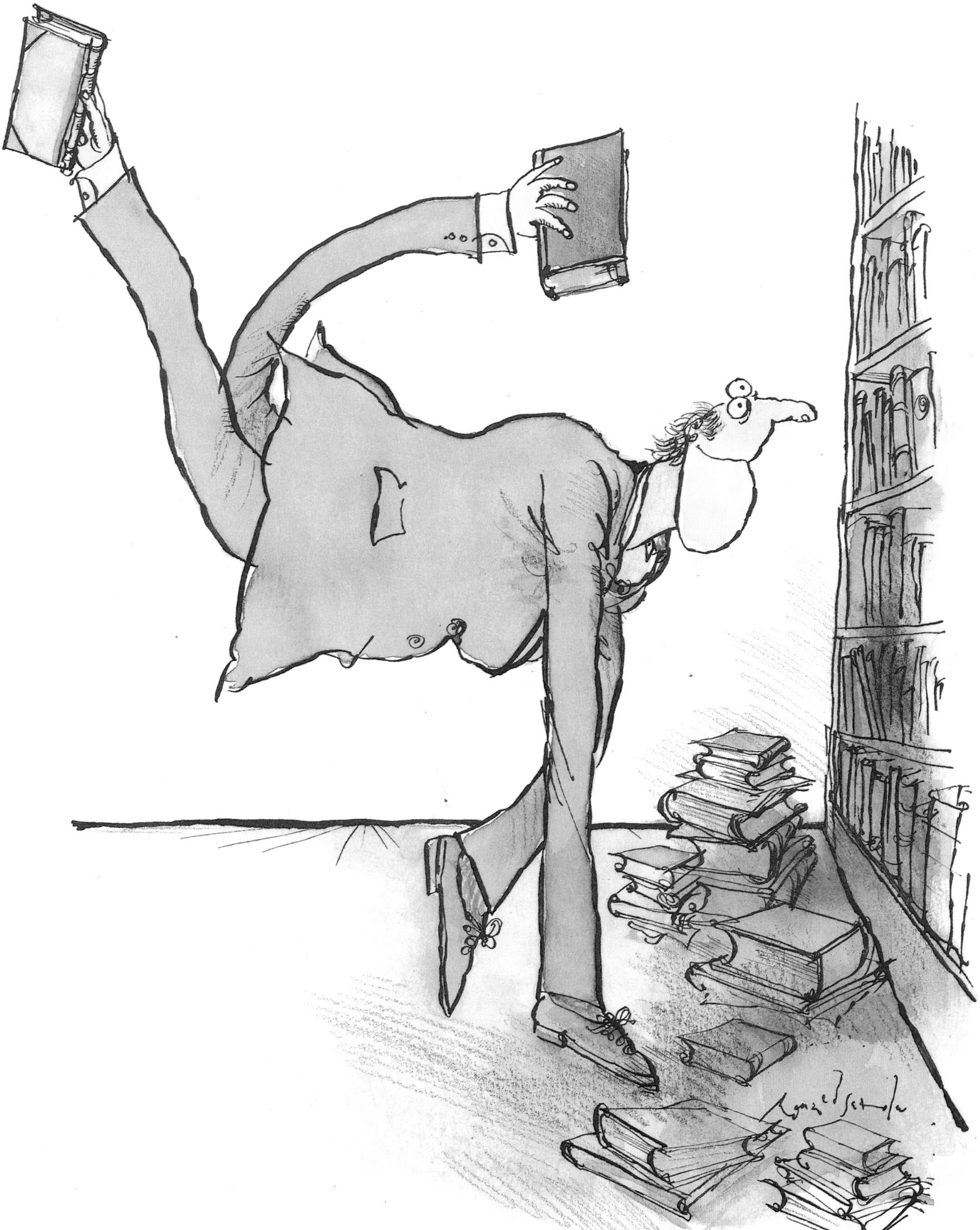

Name on fly

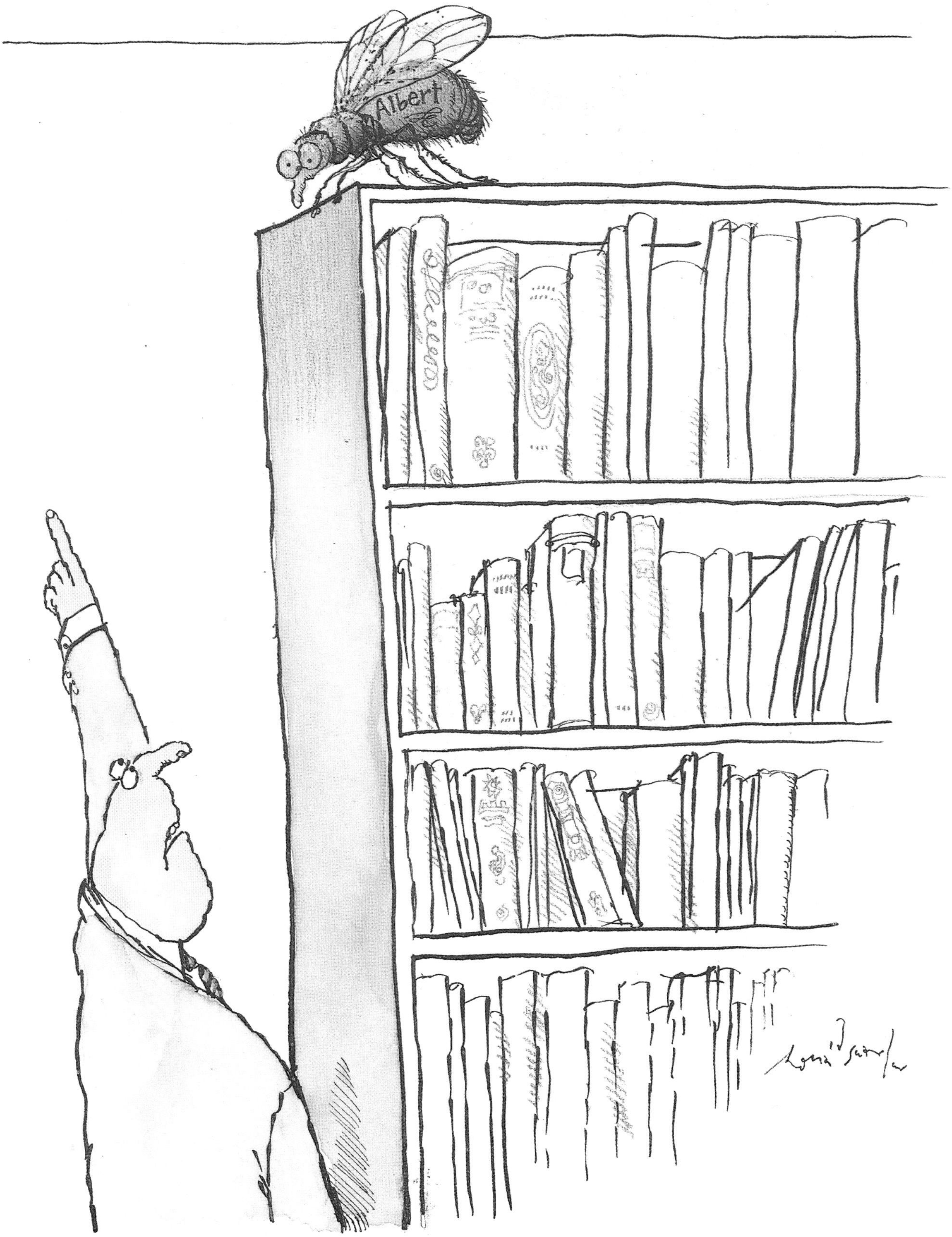
Albert

A lovely mellow copy

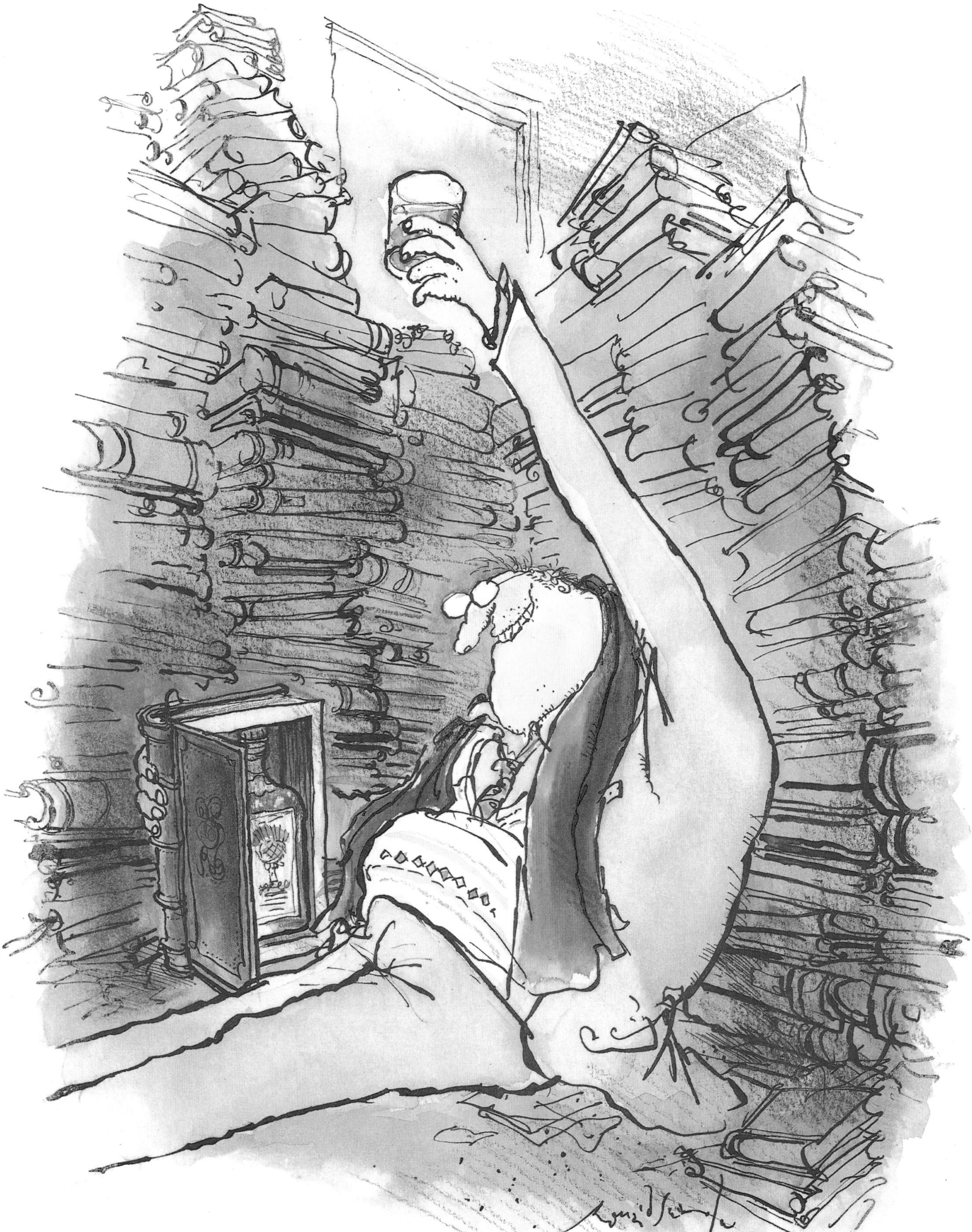

Full sheep of indeterminate age

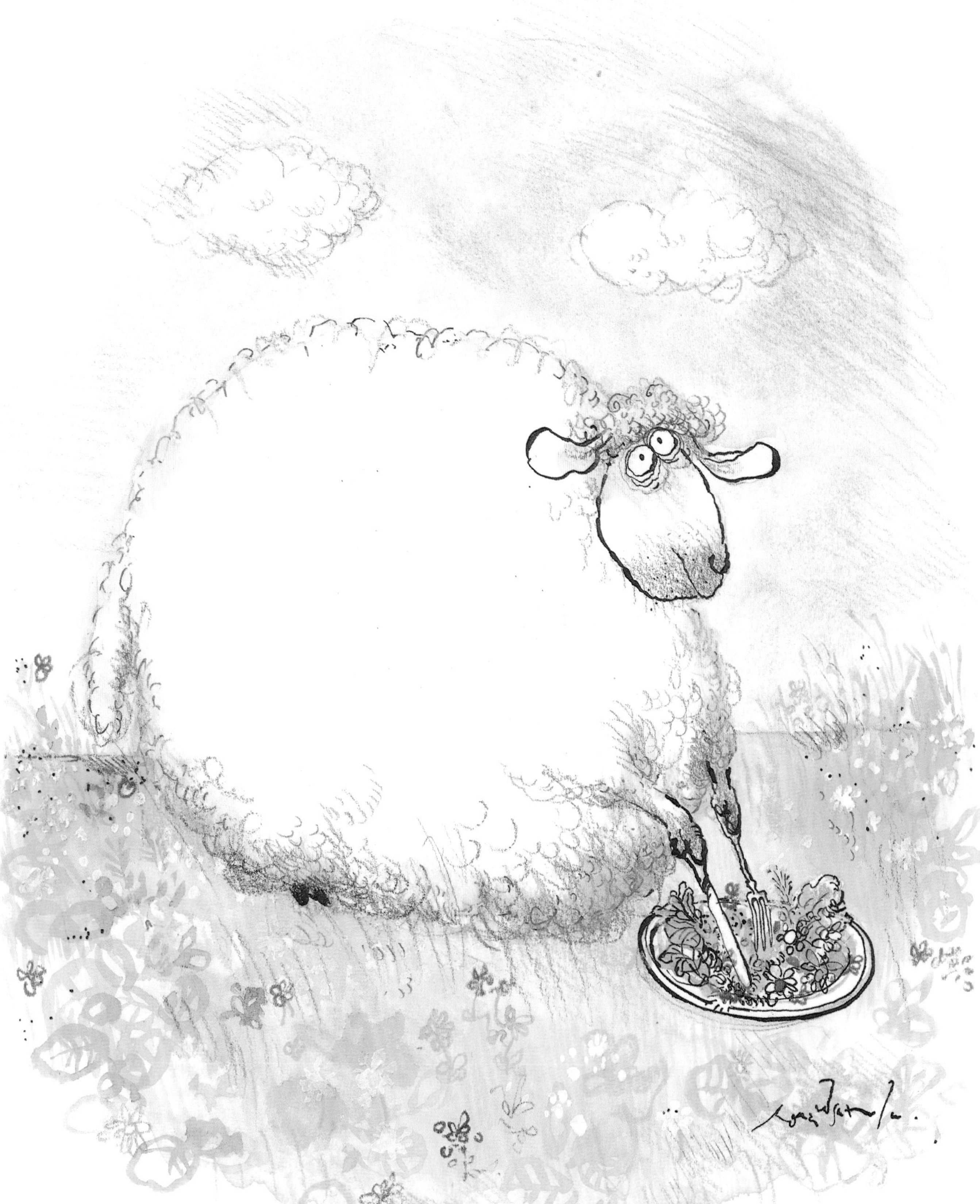

Leather labels and intricate decoration

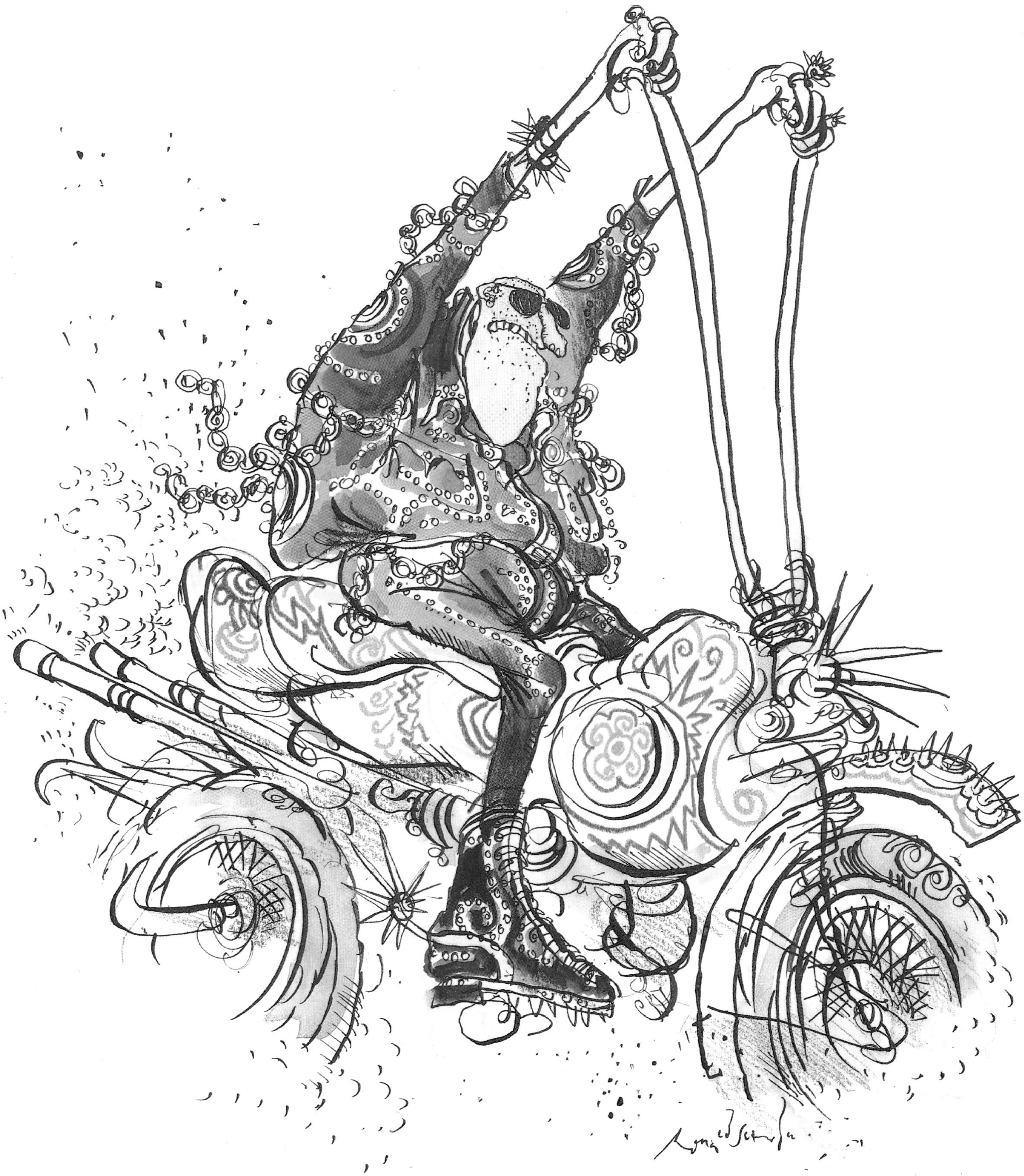

Somewhat spotted, but otherwise desirable

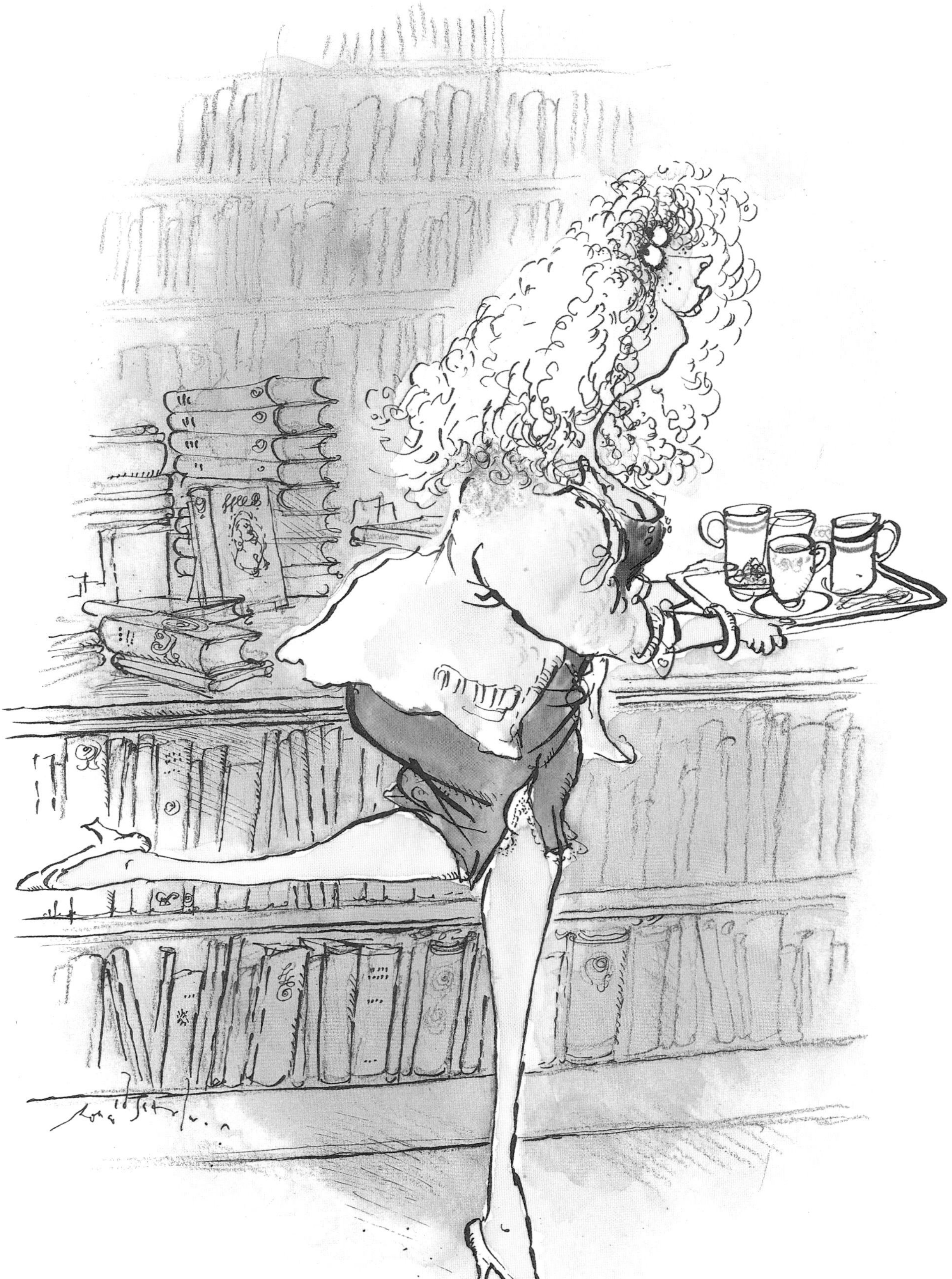

Later note of ownership

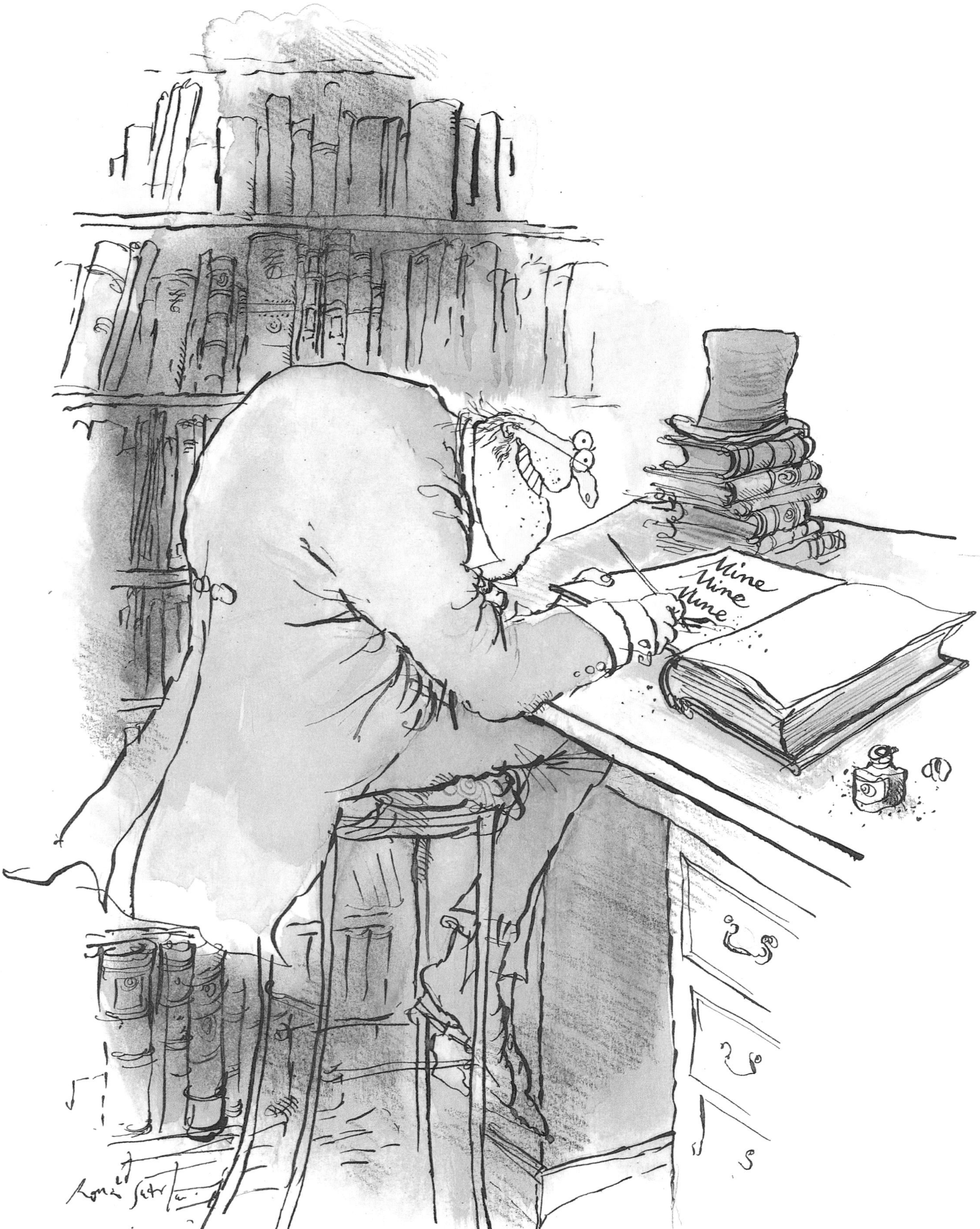
Mine
Mine
Mine

Trimmed short

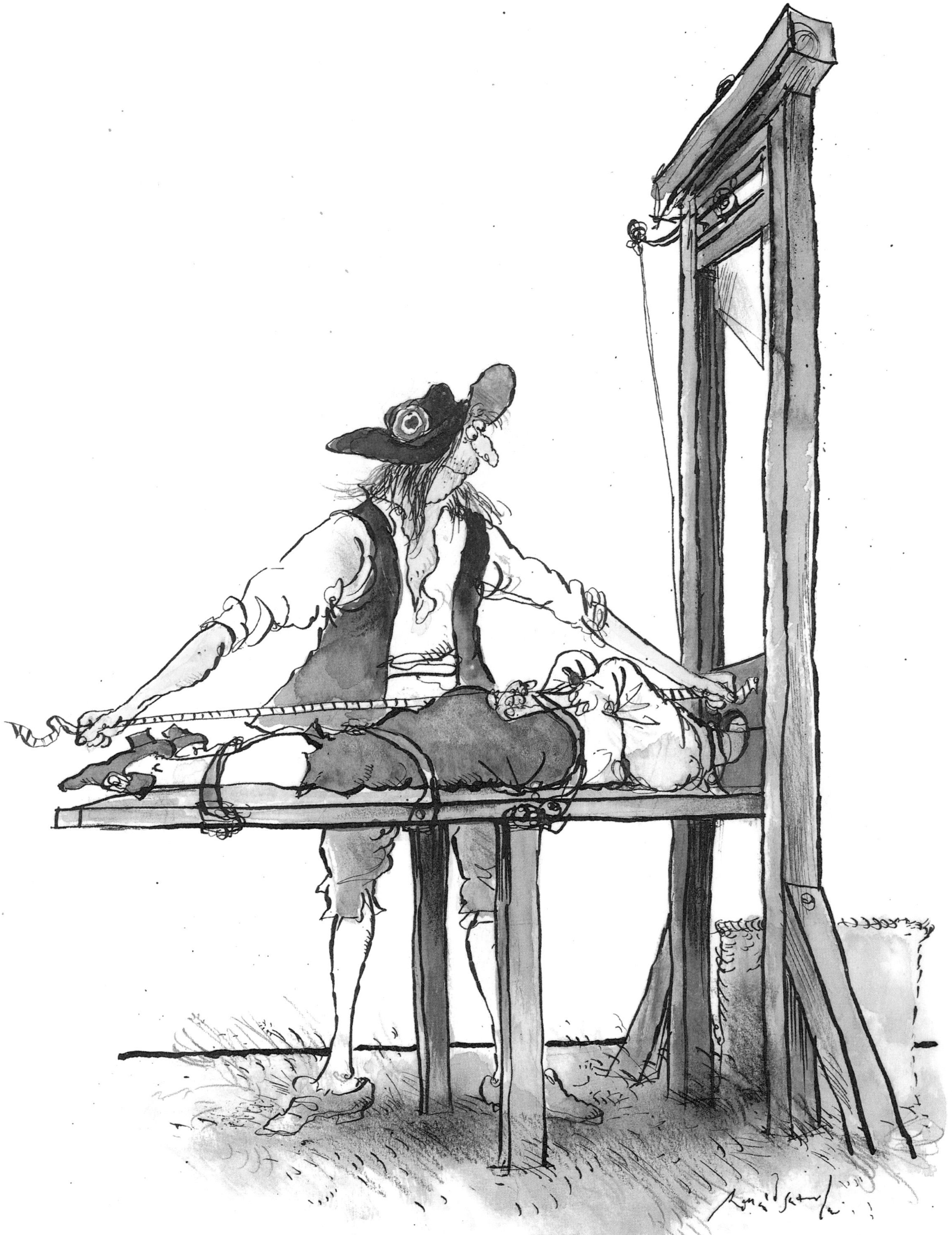

Some minor faults, otherwise in excellent
and entirely unsophisticated state

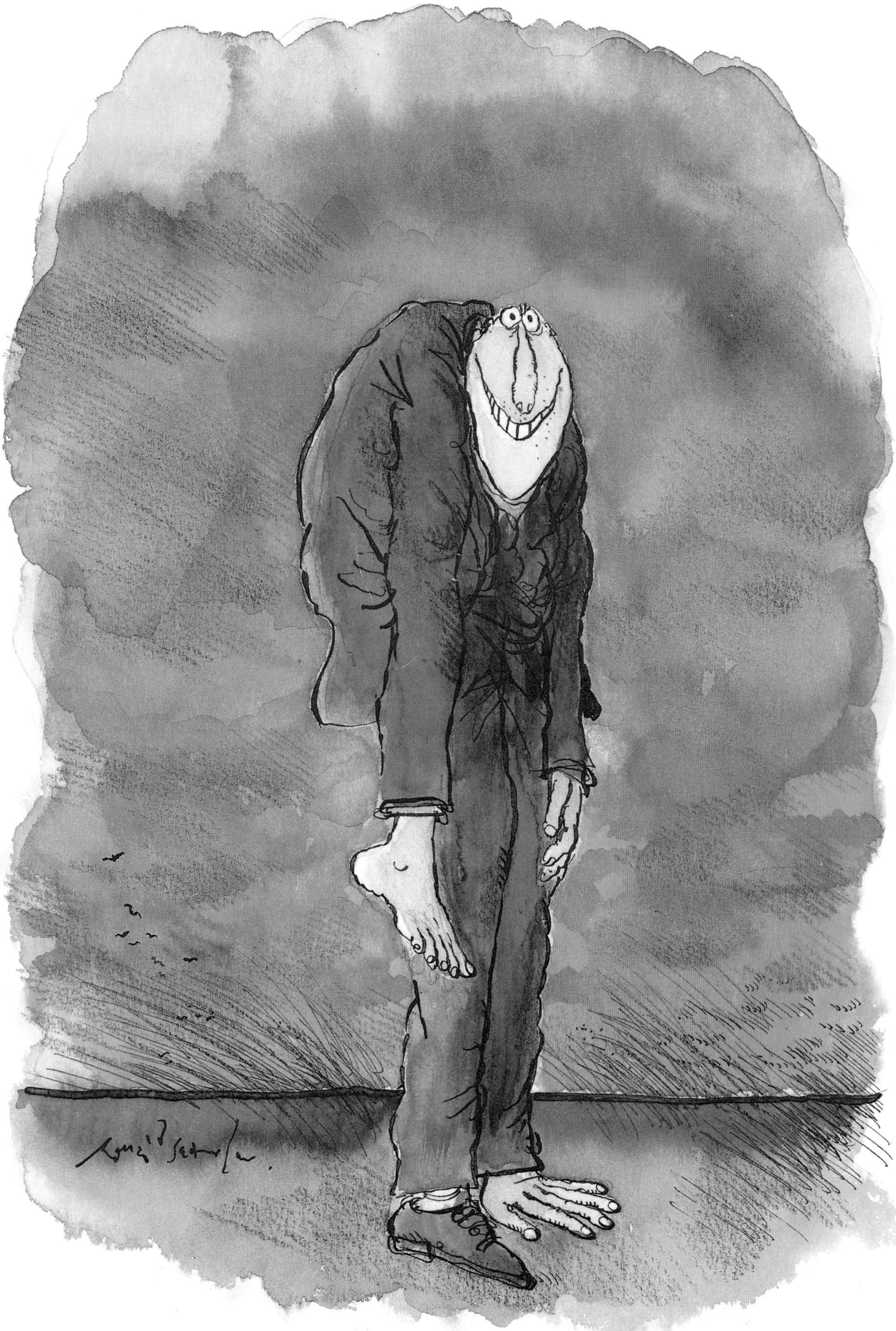

Some light surface abrasion

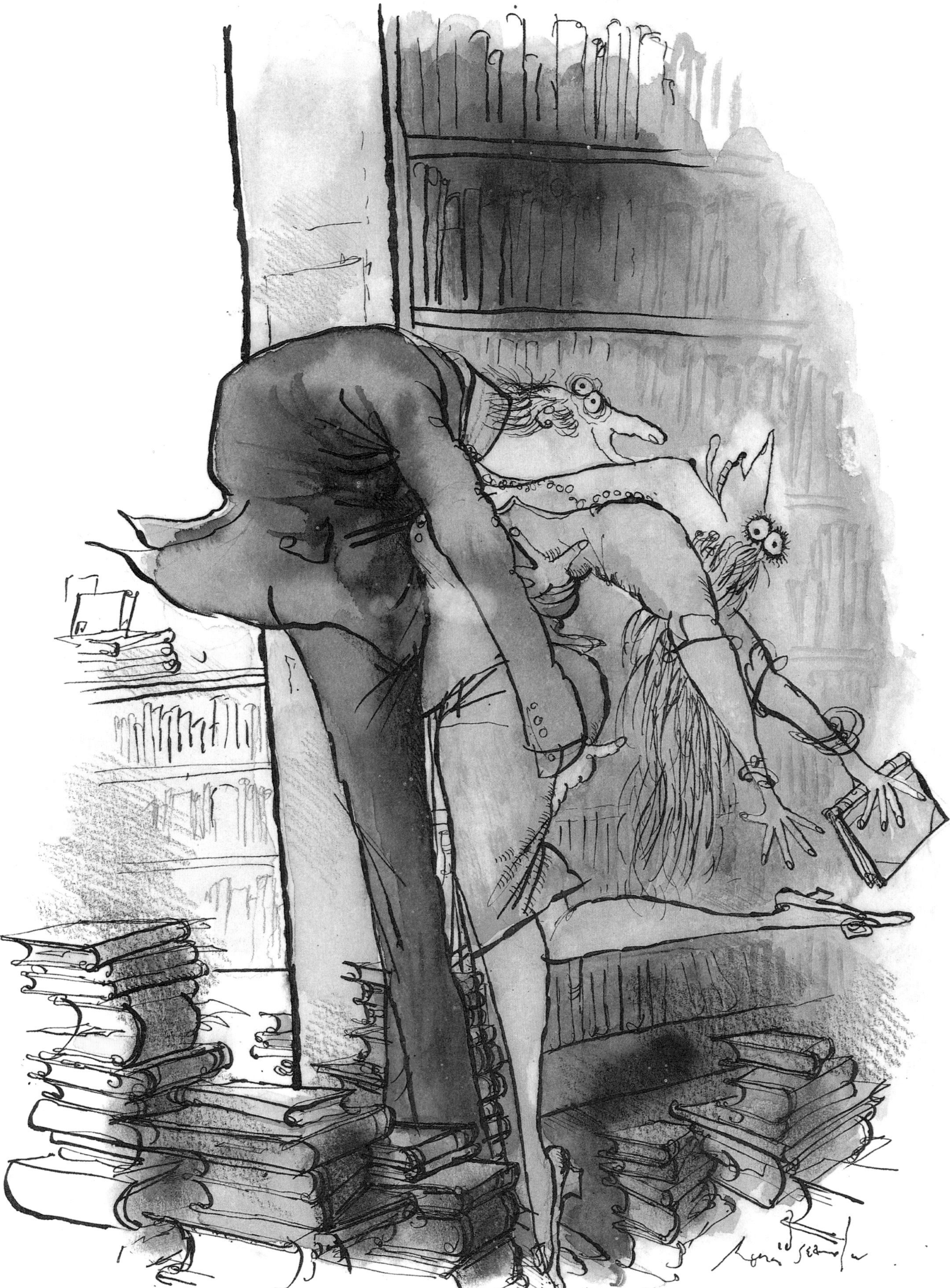

Author identified in ink on title-page

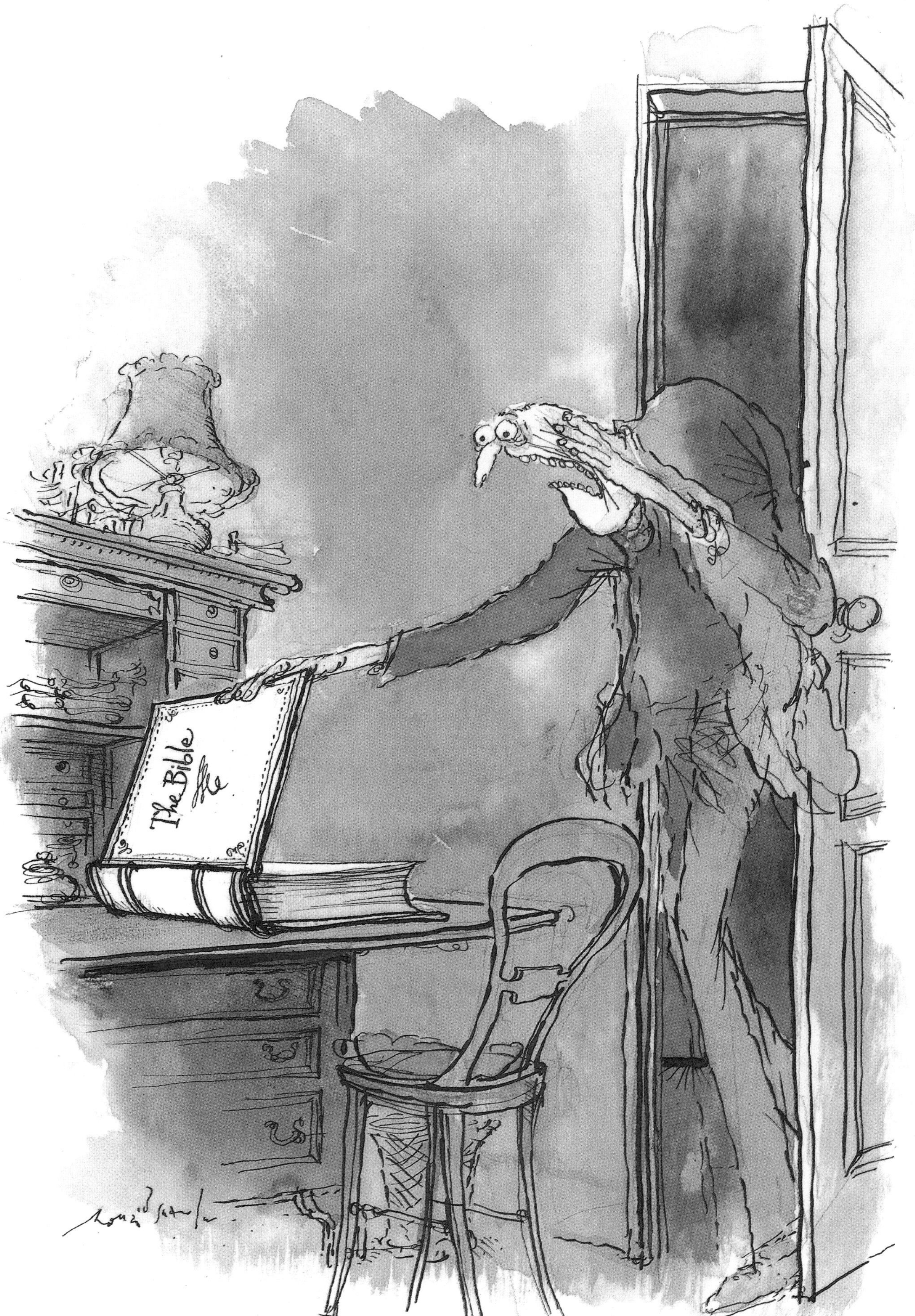
The Bible

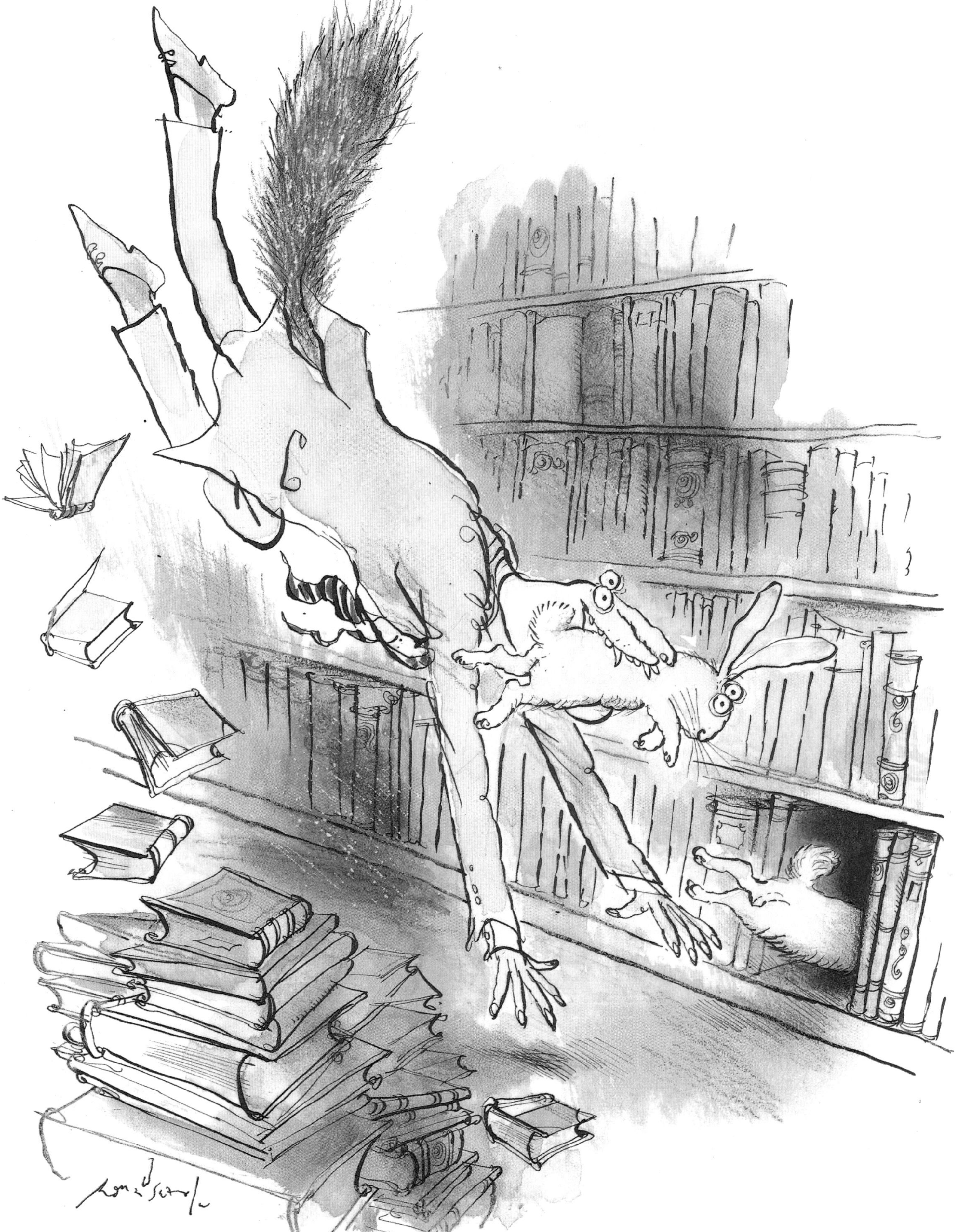

GLOSSARY

Barked	Skin scraped, rubbed, or chewed by the dog of a previous owner.
Blind-tooled	Decorations impressed on book covers without gold leaf, to save a penny or two.
B.M.	British Museum, London, a well-known catalogue house.
Calf, old style	Fine leather binding made from non-battery calf skin.
Cloth, original	What is now left of what was once a cloth binding.
Cracked (but holding)	Binding held by a thread.
Cracking	Binding held by two threads.
Decorations, intricate	Hand tooled designs impressed on binding, usually enhanced with gold leaf, by a bookbinder who did not know when to stop.
Desirable	Just about worth the money, if you *must* have it.
Disbound	Taken apart and now it's your problem.
Dog-eared	Moth-eaten, shabby and/or corners of pages turned down by some barbarian.
Extremities rubbed	Battered cardboard sticking through the corners of the binding.
Fabric tie	String used to close covers with a knot— preferably a bow—unless you have long nails.
Faults, minor	Generally messy, with traces of previous owner's breakfast.
Fly	Blank leaf at each end of a book, no buttons or zip.
Foxed	Some pages discoloured with brown damp spots.
Foxed, somewhat	Simply smothered in brown damp spots.
Foxed throughout	Needs only four legs and a tail to complete.
Headpiece	Decoration at the head of a chapter to help bump out the text.
Head, dented	Volume that has been used to replace the leg of a sideboard.
Labels	Title, author, publisher info pasted onto spine and which eventually drops off.

Loose	Stitching unravelling, signatures hanging out.
Maggs, de Nobele, Quaritch, Elte, Parikian, Wormser, Pedersen, Magee, Grant	Only American Express Gold Cards accepted.
Mellow	Distinct signs of wear, but will hold until customer is out of shop.
Morocco, pseudo	Modest binding trying to disguise itself as fine soft leather made from goatskin tanned with sumac.
Notes, later	Boring manuscript exclamations penned some time after the original date of publication by a literary thug.
Notes, manuscript	Incredibly boring comments scribbled all over the place.
Notes, marginal	Incredibly boring comments, but at least confined to the edges.
Paste-downs	Outer blank leaf of a book pasted to the inside covers to hide the joins.
Roan	Soft sheepskin leather with a close grain and no sign of hooves.
Russia	Smooth, dyed calfskin treated with birch-bark oil by a vodka-soaked serf.
Russia, half	Smooth, dyed calfskin half treated with birch-bark oil by a totally soaked serf.
Running title	Title repeated *ad nauseam* at the top of every page in case the purchaser should forget what he is reading.
Restored, ingeniously	Considerable effort made to conceal substantial faults.
Set, nice bright	Three or four moth-eaten but matching volumes in varying states of dilapidation.
Set, pleasant	Three or four matching volumes littered with biscuit crumbs, bus tickets and enough fingerprints to attract the attention of Scotland Yard.
Shaved	The binder's guillotine has converted 'y's to 'v's on every bottom line of text.
Sheep	Leather from the unconsumed parts of an unfortunate beast, or parchment of its skin.

Sheep, full	A once well-fed animal now spread over cardboard to hold pages together.
Sheep, contemporary	An ancient binding that looks as if it has been served up straight from the pot.
Signature	Large sheet of paper folded into a number of pages to become a section of a book until manhandled.
Spotted, somewhat	Splashed, stained, soiled, sullied and blemished beyond belief.
Sprung	Binding yielding in all directions.
Stitching loose	Signatures dangling.
Surface abrasion, some	Covers gouged, chewed and apparently sandpapered by a four-year-old.
Tail-edge shaved	A book's bottom adjusted to fit a high cut bathing costume.
Thumbed	Well and truly fingered.
Trimmed short	Margins unfeelingly trimmed during (re)binding and much beauty defiled, so to speak.
Unsophisticated state	As knocked together by a local printer and binder.
Unwashed	Unbleached and still human.
Washed	Foxing, soiling, contemporary kipper stains and all character removed from the paper.
Working copy	Filthy but just about decipherable.
Worming	Insect fast food stop.